THE NOOSE of SAMUEL BURROWS

For my loving family

THE NOOSE of SAMUEL BURROWS

TALES OF A NINETEENTH CENTURY HANGMAN and THOSE HE CONDEMNED

NICK KEVERN

First published in Great Britain in 2025 by
PEN AND SWORD TRUE CRIME
An imprint of
Pen & Sword Books Ltd
Yorkshire – Philadelphia

Copyright © Nick Kevern, 2025

ISBN 978 1 03611 070 3

The right of Nick Kevern to be identified as Author of this work has been asserted by him in accordance with the Copyright, Designs and Patents Act 1988.

A CIP catalogue record for this book is available from the British Library.

All rights reserved. No part of this book may be reproduced, transmitted, downloaded, decompiled or reverse engineered in any form or by any means, electronic or mechanical including photocopying, recording or by any information storage and retrieval system, without permission from the Publisher in writing.
NO AI TRAINING: Without in any way limiting the Author's and Publisher's exclusive rights under copyright, any use of this publication to "train" generative artificial intelligence (AI) technologies to generate text is expressly prohibited.
The Author and Publisher reserve all rights to license uses of this work for generative AI training and development of machine learning language models.

Typeset in Times New Roman 12/16 by SJmagic DESIGN SERVICES, India.
Printed and bound in the UK by CPI Group (UK) Ltd, Croydon, CR0 4YY.

The Publisher's authorised representative in the EU for product safety is Authorised Rep Compliance Ltd., Ground Floor, 71 Lower Baggot Street, Dublin D02 P593, Ireland. www.arccompliance.com

For a complete list of Pen & Sword titles please contact
PEN & SWORD BOOKS LIMITED
George House, Units 12 & 13, Beevor Street, Off Pontefract Road,
Barnsley, South Yorkshire, S71 1HN, England
E-mail: enquiries@pen-and-sword.co.uk
Website: www.pen-and-sword.co.uk

or

PEN AND SWORD BOOKS
1950 Lawrence Rd, Havertown, PA 19083, USA
E-mail: uspen-and-sword@casematepublishers.com
Website: www.penandswordbooks.com

Contents

Acknowledgements vii

Author's Note viii

Chapter 1   The Hangman's Burden 1

Chapter 2   Life Before the Noose 9

Chapter 3   The Men Who Dropped Twice 15

Chapter 4   A Done Deal 26

Chapter 5   Rage Against the Machines 32

Chapter 6   A Very Public Ordeal 41

Chapter 7   The Tragedy of Miss Porter 56

Chapter 8   This Time It's Personal 61

Chapter 9   The Devil's Bank Notes 73

Chapter 10   The Road to Near Ruin 83

Chapter 11   Five Days Racing and a Hanging 93

Chapter 12   On the Road Again 98

Chapter 13   Dead Man's Clothes 104

Chapter 14   The Changing Tide 113

Chapter 15   The Curious Case of Charles Burrows 122

Chapter 16	The Hangman's Idle Hands	130
Chapter 17	Tears of the Hangman	134
Chapter 18	When the Hangman Came to Beaumaris	141
Chapter 19	The Hat on the Wye	150
Chapter 20	The Swinger Rioters	159
Chapter 21	The Final Dance of Death	168
Chapter 22	Fading Away	175
Notes		182
Bibliography		198
Index		206

Acknowledgements

I WOULD LIKE to sincerely thank everyone who has been a part of this book in one way or another. The staff at the Chester Record Offices have been faultless in their desire to help me gather as much as they possibly could relating to the life and times of Samuel Burrows. Without your professionalism and enthusiasm, this would not have been possible. I would also like to thank the staff at the British Library, National Archives, North East Wales Archives and Shropshire Archives for all their help in gathering the necessary records for me.

The support of Trevor Summerhill at Ye Olde Cottage in Chester will never be forgotten during this time and I have enjoyed all of our talks regarding the book. I would also like to take this opportunity to thank Steve Howe and Rob Hayes for their constant support and efforts in helping me to ensure that this book was completed. I would also like to thank the staff at the Cross Keys who hosted the event that led to the writing of this book.

Writing a book is far from a straightforward affair. For this reason I am indebted to Amy Jordan at Pen & Sword books for commissioning *The Noose of Samuel Burrows*. Your guidance and support has been greatly appreciated throughout. I am also grateful for the work of Jon Wilkinson who has produced an amazing and eye-catching cover and Paul Middleton, my editor, for going through this book with a fine toothcomb.

Finally I would like to thank my family and friends who have supported me throughout the writing of this book and helped to keep me sane, especially Gracie Clarke. Without the love and support of Gracie, this book would simply not have happened in the first place. Your constant encouragement has meant everything to me.

Author's Note

IF THE NAME of Samuel Burrows is unfamiliar to you then don't despair. You are not alone.

Samuel Burrows did nothing significant. He never won major battles, never held a high office, and never made decisions that impacted a country. In the era of Georgian Britain, he was simply no one. Like many, his primary aim was to survive by any means necessary as inflation and war ravaged the country. With the whiff of revolution in the air, it would be men like Samuel Burrows who were used as a weapon of fear to those contemplating a revolt. For hardened criminals, his pounding footsteps would be the last they would hear. For the innocent, caught up in the legal wranglings of the country's 'Bloody Code', his face would be the last that they would see before they were blinded by the hood he placed over their head.

Burrows would often state that it was nothing personal as he pulled the lever that would send many into eternity. Their crimes meant little to him so long as he got paid. Soon, like most things in life, the money became all that mattered to him.

As an early nineteenth-century hangman, Burrows witnessed change at first hand and those that he executed ranged from those who committed a simple mistake of desperation to those who murdered for love. Those who revolted against the excessive changes to the country and the highwaymen who stole from others.

It was also a time of judicial progress that affected Burrows directly. The so-called 'Bloody Code' ensured that nearly 220 crimes were punishable by death, which meant that Burrows was a busy man. However, he would

Author's Note

see his profession suffer as reforms were introduced to reduce the need for his grizzly rope.

In many respects, this is the Georgian world that you may not have come across. The gala balls where the rich danced and ate heartily are not to be seen here. Instead, the working-class Georgian story is one about survival where sometimes the reward of criminality outweighed the risk.

As the Georgian era came to an end, so too did the era of public execution and before long the hysteria of crowds gathering to watch someone die vanished. For the men who completed this horrific task, the burden was great but the riches were greatly received. The work would see Burrows perform executions not only in his home town of Chester but travel to Beaumaris, Carnarvon (now Caernarfon), Hereford, Shrewsbury and Ruthin.

Despite this, Burrows is rarely mentioned even in the city which he once called home. For a man who enjoyed his own celebrity, the city hardly recalls his name. It would be in the archives where this man would see out his memory, waiting for the moment for someone to remember him and remind people of who he really was.

While a biography of Burrows is all but impossible, it is feasible to look at his life in considerable detail through the stories of those who faced him during their final moments on the earth. From the surgeons who performed dissections, to the public houses who regularly served him, it is possible to reveal more about Georgian Chester through the eyes of those who called the place home.

You might not have known who Burrows was before you opened this book but soon you will know him, and those who he condemned, in ways you never imagined. History might have forgotten about Samuel Burrows for so long but now is the time to reawaken a story from the past.

Chapter 1

The Hangman's Burden

Brook Street, Chester, October 1835

SAMUEL BURROWS WAS all alone. The flickering embers of his fireplace were his only companion as the crackling flames filled the room with its only noise. His wife, Mary, had passed away months earlier and with this firmly on his mind, he knew that it was only a matter of time before he would be joining her. The abdominal pains that he was feeling had intensified due to a liver complaint that he was experiencing and were made even worse as he began to drink himself into oblivion.[1] While it was indeed true that Samuel had spent the vast majority of his later life in a state of inebriation, he had recently taken it to a whole different level since his wife's passing. Like the fire that lay in front of him, he knew everything would eventually fade over time and eventually burn out. Samuel was no different.

The intense pain had left him practically bed bound in his Brook Street abode as the world continued to turn around him. While he could still move around, he did so sparingly in order to preserve any remaining energy that he still had. The fatigue had taken its hold on him once again as the last life of the fire was beginning to burn out. Above the fire was his only portrait. It was a portrait of himself from what he perceived to be better times. Rather than an old man in poor health struggling to stay warm on the chilly October night, it reminded him about how proudly he once stood. It was a time when his name was known throughout the county of Cheshire as the people of the City of Chester eagerly watched his every move.

The Noose of Samuel Burrows

In Samuel's eyes, he was an important man within Cestrian circles. It was why he had his crude silhouette portrait made in the first place. Looking at his portrait, he remembered heading to 51 Bridge Street Row in order to have it made. It was here where a small group of artists from London had arrived creating what they called 'likenesses'; a silhouette-based drawing using the side of the sitter's face. Once that silhouette was drawn, the artist would then add further details but on the whole it gave the sitter a crude likeness to take away for themselves.[2]

The portrait had cost Burrows 1 shilling and came complete with glass and frame, which he mounted proudly on the wall of his Brook Street residence. Burrows recalled the excitement on the faces of the artists when he revealed who he was. Knowing that a local celebrity was in attendance, the artists asked for his consent for the image to be used for some further promotion of their tour schedule. Needless to say, the thought of his image being used in the local press filled Burrows with joy. Of course, they could use it.

His image would later appear in the *Chester Courant* on 29 August 1826, in order to promote the artist's visit to the city. Burrows loved nothing more than seeing his face, albeit the side of his face, in the papers. Underneath his image, it simply stated 'Sammy Burrows, the Executioner of the City'.[3]

For Samuel, it was one of the few times that people did not recoil in fear when he stated what he did for a living. Many around him knew exactly who he was. He was the 'finisher of the law' who unleashed the ultimate punishment on condemned criminals. He was loathed and feared in equal measure by the general public, but in Samuel's eyes he was simply a cog in the wheel of the kingdom's system of justice. Yet, it was a job that he fulfilled brazenly and without remorse. The law was the law in his mind and he gratefully received the riches of his hangman's wage.

The younger man who he remembered as the flames were slowly dying was far from the man he was at this particular moment of time. Now he was beginning to wonder what was to become of him. Questions surrounding forgiveness began to race around his mind as this once notorious, hardened man was clinging to life. His approaching demise had made him think about his life in ways he had never thought of it before. Would the gates of heaven be open to him or would the eternal damnation of the flames that he was currently staring at take his soul?

He felt yet another throbbing in his stomach. The pain was so intense that he huddled over, eager to vomit yet nothing was coming from his mouth. He reached over for some ale and gulped it down. The thirst grew ever more and no matter how much he consumed it couldn't be fully quenched. Drinking had always been a part of Samuel's life, and now it was helping to end it too.

There was a loud crackle from the fire as the remaining wood began to split. In his mind, it sounded similar to the crowds that used to attend his executions at the New City Gaol. Burrows closed his eyes in a vain attempt to visualise them. Crowds stretching in their thousands would come from all around the county of Cheshire to see him at work. Some of his performances he could remember vividly, while others were blurred by the alcohol he consumed prior to the execution.

As he stood on top of the gates of the New City Gaol he could hear the wood wince beneath his feet with every step he took. Looking around him he could see the multitude of people. He remembered the look on their faces as the condemned dropped beneath him. While some were shocked by the events happening before their eyes, others cheered, almost salivating with joy at the macabre performance that they were witnessing. Burrows began to chuckle as he remembered placing his own head in the noose and mimicking the impending death of the condemned. While some would laugh as he did this, others were quick to show their disdain for him. Seeing this in his mind, it finally dawned on him that he was an acquired taste.

The portrait above the fire was beginning to fade out of his sight as the flames were quickly running out of oxygen. It was something that would eventually happen to us all, Burrows thought to himself, as he began to wonder more and more about his final breath. Burrows began to think about those who he took that final breath away from. As the condemned dropped, Burrows would encourage even more cheers as the crowd went wild. The aim was that the fall and the placement of the noose behind the head of the victim would see an instant death, but Burrows did not always allow that to happen. For him, sensationalism was all part of the performance. For many of those he executed, it would be a slower, more agonising death as their neck failed to break. Instead, they would find themselves slowly strangled and struggling high above the crowd in a futile effort to prolong their life. Once the final shake was complete and their soul departed their body, Burrows would leave them there for up to an hour. When it came to professionalism, Burrows was the kind of man who saw the satisfaction of the crowd as more important than the condemned's final moments of humility.

Burrows remembered the reprimands that he received. The calls for more professionalism were not restricted to the powers that be but also from the press and the crowd itself. Burrows, however, laughed them off; after all, the criminals were dead and therefore he had completed his job.

Another drink was needed to ease his prolonged cough. He reached around but the dying flickers of the fire had brought the room to near darkness. Burrows let out a curse as he knocked his drink over. As it spilled into the wooden beams, he knew that he would have to go without until the morning. But he still was not ready to sleep no matter how tired he was.

Somehow his life had always revolved around the idea of death. Whether it was to execute condemned criminals or during his previous life as a butcher. The carcass, the stillness of it all. Although the animal was already dead, there was a striking similarity to those who he saw hang after the last ebbs of life frittered away. Butchery ran through his veins. It had been a part of his life for as long as he could remember ever since he served as an apprentice in Ravensmoor. Moving to Chester in the late eighteenth century, he quickly found work in the Shambles area of Chester on Northgate Street working in the makeshift wooden shacks that filled the area around the Exchange in Market Square. It was hard, gruelling work with long hours. The money that he made was simply not stretching far enough anymore as his family grew.

The Hangman's Burden

His family had become a distant shadow and yet he began to think of them right now. There was, of course, a reason as to why no one was there for him when he needed them the most. From the moment Mary passed away, he knew he was all alone. His oldest son Henry had died in service in the East Indies but he had a feeling that his youngest son Charles was still alive and well. There was, however, no time for Charles to see his dying father. He was in Van Diemen's Land (now Tasmania) on the other side of the world. Charles would be another consequence that Samuel now had plenty of time to think about.[4]

The darkness had finally arrived. With it came the shadows of the fifty-three souls that Burrows had joyfully sent to meet their maker.[5] Each one had their own stories to tell, their own reasons for walking up the rickety steps and up the gallows to face the man who would soon send them into eternity. While Burrows cared little to hear them, the darkness heightened his senses and it consumed him. He clung to the notion that they were destined to face him due to the crimes that they had committed, but in reality even Burrows knew that it really was not that simple. No matter how he tried to justify it, he had still taken a life and for that reason he needed to repent.

Thankfully he knew that once the morning arrived the Reverend William Clarke would be here. Only then could he find the Lord's forgiveness. Until then though, he needed to sleep, no matter how much the shadows of the condemned wouldn't let him. Hopefully, in repenting his sins, the Lord would release the hangman from his burden.[6]

It was all but dark in Samuel Burrows' bedroom by the time the Reverend Clarke arrived. Prompt as always, he arrived ahead of time, much to Samuel's annoyance. Burrows had left the door unlocked for his arrival and as Clarke opened the bedroom door he could see the state that Burrows was in. He went to open the curtains to let the morning sun in and as he did he saw the disturbed dust dance around the room. Burrows remained in bed but as Clarke ventured towards him he knocked Burrows' chamber pot and stale urine spilled on to the floor. As he looked around, he could clearly see the room was in much need of a clean but knowing that Burrows' wife had passed away the previous March, he realised there was little anyone could do for him. For now, all Clarke could do was to provide a little Christian charity, empty the chamber pot, and fetch some much-needed water. Burrows let out a groan as his intestinal pain once again resurfaced. Clarke wouldn't be long gathering some essentials for the sickly man that lay before him.

The two men had known each other for some time dating back to Clarke's time at New City Gaol, where he provided religious comfort to those about to face Burrows' noose.[7] Whatever Clarke really thought of Burrows, he decided to keep it to himself. However, it would be fair to say that Clarke was not a fan of Burrows' antics, especially when it came to his behaviour on top of the gallows. Now he found himself on Brook Street preparing to give religious comfort to the man who launched so many into eternity. Returning with water alongside some bread and cheese, he saw the hangman painfully attempt to get himself out of bed. Burrows couldn't muster the strength to get up properly and promptly fell back. Slightly concerned for his well-being, Clarke placed what he had gathered on to a dusty table and rushed towards him. As he approached Burrows, Clarke could see all too well that he was not long for this world. Time was running out for the hangman.

The two men spoke about their time at New City Gaol, with Burrows almost returning to his old self as he did, recanting memories of those they both knew well. Burrows highlighted that those he condemned broke the law and therefore he had little to repent. However, Clarke was not here to regale his host with stories and was quick to remind Burrows that his eventual place in the kingdom of heaven was not guaranteed based solely on the law of the land. He still had to repent his sins. The condemned and the burden that Burrows felt were in some way entwined in Clarke's mind. Only through the act of forgiveness in the eyes of the Lord could the hangman be truly saved.

The Hangman's Burden

With Burrows reluctant to ask for forgiveness, Clarke began to read scriptures from the Bible in order to educate him further. As Clarke opened the book, Burrows stared intently towards the reverend. He began with Matthew Chapter 6, verses 14–15 to remind Burrows that a place in heaven was still salvageable for him.

Clarke read the passage out aloud: 'For if ye forgive men their trespasses, your heavenly Father will also forgive you: But if ye forgive not men their trespasses, neither will your Father forgive your trespasses.'

Burrows was in deep thought thinking about those words. He had never thought too much about those that would end up on the other end of his noose at the time, but with his own end now quickly approaching, it was beginning to weigh heavily on his mind. Clarke informed Samuel that when reading from the scriptures it was this passage that always had the most effect on the condemned as they were about to face their executioner. Burrows laughed, informing the reverend that their spirits still haunted him and had done for years. If they forgave him, then why did they still haunt him?

Clarke breathed out a sigh. He was finally getting through to the stubborn hangman. The reverend continued to explain that it was because he buried his sin away with drink rather than asking for forgiveness from the Lord. Only then could he truly be free. Burrows nodded with reluctant agreement.

Clarke urged him to look back over his life and ask for forgiveness but reminded him that it had to be sincere as the Lord would know. It had to be genuine remorse. As Clarke was about to turn the page in order to find another example that could help, Burrows placed his hand on the Bible. Clarke looked at him, closed the book, and placed it in the hangman's firm grip. Burrows was about to talk about his life as the city's executioner in the faint hope that he could redeem his soul in the eyes of the Lord. Clarke got Burrows a drink and then sat down beside him. He was ready to listen and hoped that the Lord was listening too.

As Burrows began to reveal his story to the reverend, he looked once again at the portrait of himself above the fireplace. With the light of the new morning once again filling the room, it was clearer for him to see his younger self. Now he saw a man filled with arrogance and pride in what he did rather than a man begging for forgiveness. He had never thought about those condemned souls as he pulled on his lever, and if he ever did, it was fleeting. Now, the time was right. Forgiveness was for the Lord to decide. All he could do was to tell Clarke as much as he could, and pray that God was listening to every word.

Chapter 2

Life Before the Noose

SAMUEL BURROWS WAS no one extraordinary. It is perhaps for this reason that he has become all but forgotten, even in the city where he once lived. For a man like Burrows, survival was realistically the only thing about his life that could be called any form of ambition. He was simply a lower working-class man who just so happened to live at a time of seismic change within Britain. Yet, rather unwittingly, he had a front-row seat during this time of change, and those who he encountered on his journey of life all had their own stories to tell. The only difference between them and him was that it would be Burrows himself who condemned them to their untimely deaths.

Burrows roamed the streets of the City of Chester during the late eighteenth and early nineteenth centuries. It was an era of warfare, protest, revolt, poverty, and more importantly for him, crime. Burrows found himself inadvertently involved with all of the above in some way, shape or form. He was an ostracised member of Cestrian society, a bogeyman of sorts who was loathed as well as feared. Naturally, he never saw himself in that same way. Instead, he viewed himself as a vital cog in the wheels of British justice. He was not, in any way, skilled or even exceptional in his work. Anyone who had the stomach to do what he did could have easily done the same job that he did. He was a brutish man and was never one to shy away from a fight, especially when heavily intoxicated with alcohol, which was often.[1] He was far from any kind of role model, and any respect that he might have earned during his earlier life was swiftly eroded when he took on the post that he was best remembered for.

The Noose of Samuel Burrows

Those who stumbled upon him as he carried out his duties would have met him all but briefly. Yet the reasons for their eventual encounter with Burrows highlighted the severe disparities within Georgian society. From those who were just trying to survive the daily bleakness of their situations, to those who were fighting against the system that they believed was holding them back; Burrows met them all. He was the final part of a justice system in arguably the most bloody era of them all. He was the finisher of the law and he performed his work with gusto, showing little remorse. Those who faced him in the City of Chester when he was on official duty were facing the last man they would ever see.

Why they were facing him was of no concern to Burrows.

Like many who arrived in Chester in the late eighteenth century, Samuel Burrows simply appeared from nowhere. He was born in Ravensmoor, a small rural village just outside the town of Nantwich, on 28 June 1772 but much of his early life is all but a mystery and undocumented.[2] What we do know though is that the small hamlet could never truly hold the scale of his ambition. Even as a young man, Samuel desired to be noticed and appreciated much more than the confines of Ravensmoor could ever give him.

With the idea of a national census still a dream, we do not know exactly when he entered the City of Chester, but once he arrived he firmly established himself. Previously trained as a butcher, Burrows quickly sought work in the Northgate Street Shambles. Burrows established himself within his new community with relative ease and it was in the busy streets of Chester where he first met Mary Williams.

She was seven years older than Samuel, who was becoming a moderate success as a butcher in his own right, but the age difference never seemed to affect their growing relationship and affection for each other. Finding a home within Northgate Street, the pair would eventually marry on 17 November 1794.[3] At 22 years old, Samuel Burrows was now firmly a part of Cestrian life. Two surviving boys would later fill their dwellings, despite Mary previously miscarrying on a couple of occasions.

For Samuel, life was good, even despite the ordeals that the couple had to overcome. His shack on the Shambles was a busy place to work.

While an unpleasant setting to many people, Burrows was becoming an expert in his trade, as entrails and congealed blood soaked the cobbles beneath him. However, it was still not enough for an ambitious young man who believed that he was created for more than simply cutting meat for grateful customers.[4] From Mary's point of view, living with a man like Samuel had its ups and downs. His desire to be noticed often got him into trouble and each time that happened Mary would pick up the pieces.

In his desperate attempts to become more visible in the city the blurred line between infamy and likeability was crossed regularly. On one hand, Samuel was a charmer who would use his charisma to get himself out of any potential trouble. However, on the other hand, he craved authority and was equipped to physically handle any situation. Desperate to gain any influence within the city, he saw butchery as a financial means to an end as his ambitions grew.

For Mary, Samuel's constant ambition was both a source of both pride and confusion, even though she knew that some of what he said was nonsense. How could a man like Samuel possibly climb the ladder in a society that was firmly fixed? Mary simply put it all down to talk, never fully realising that Samuel would actually act on his delusions of grandeur.

In order to make his dreams a reality, Burrows would accept anything that would enable him to be known within the community. He would become the beadle for the parish of St Oswalds in the centre of the city.[5] It was an ideal role for a man like Burrows and one that suited his more authoritarian sense of himself. Every Sunday, he would gather the community to the church, eager to find anyone who opted to avoid the congregation and force them in. Once inside he would look over the pews for anyone not paying attention. Acting as an overwatcher for the Lord, determined to keep the flock in line, Burrows would soon become known as a man not to be messed with. Not because he was a religious zealot, but because he took his authority seriously.

His once happy and somewhat charming demeanour was changing to one of a frowning, serious, and at times aggressive man. That's not to say that he was not liked. Drinking would often reveal the man he once was. Funny and light-hearted with a cheeky wit, Burrows would regress to his former self if enough ale slid down his throat. It would be in the public houses of Chester where fellow Cestrians saw another side to their authoritarian beadle.

When the opportunity arose to become one of Chester's special constables, Burrows gladly accepted the position. Leaving his position as a parish beadle, Burrows now found himself stalking the streets in search of any potential criminality, and talking to local business owners about security. Often acting as a watchman for the city, Burrows would spend many nights at either the Northgate Gaol or the newly established holding cell under the columns of the City's Exchange in Market Square. The authority that Burrows craved so much was now his. In his mind, at least, he was making a difference.

Chester's need for an executioner was never really on his mind when he served as a special constable. The city had not seen a public execution in over seven years but things were about to change. Thomas Harrison was busy with his plans for the New City Gaol, which was to be built next to the infirmary. With the Northgate Gaol in a state of disrepair, the city corporation had commissioned a new building in order to suit the ever-growing population of Chester. Furthermore, Harrison had been told that the new building needed to have the ability to conduct executions high above the entrances of the gaol in order that thousands of people could witness them.[6]

The City of Chester was bringing back the spectacle of public execution, and even invested in the latest technology to make the event more efficient. The days of the short drop were over and a mobile mechanical drop was commissioned. Rather than kicking a stool in the fields of Gallows Hill or even, in the case of Aaron Gee and Thomas Gibson, being pushed out of the window at the Northgate Gaol in 1801,[7] the long drop included a trapdoor mechanism. The potential executioner would simply need to attach the noose to a high beam, place the condemned over the trapdoor and then pull the lever. Now the city needed someone who was prepared to be their new executioner.

It was never a popular position to fill. Most executioners were reluctant to take on such a role and those that did knew that at least they could hide under the guise of anonymity beneath a hood. Although a fairly well-paid job, it came with a certain amount of risk. If the community knew what you did it could quickly become a danger as the mob could easily turn on the executioner. For a man like Burrows who craved attention it did not appear to be an obvious choice of profession.

Burrows did have many of the prerequisites that were essential for this line of work. He was a hardened man with a respect for authority. More importantly, he was not squeamish in any sense given his current line of work on the Shambles. His work as a special constable also showed a man who fully believed in the process of the law and was ruthless in his quest to catch wrongdoers. As the executioner of the city, and therefore the county of Cheshire, Burrows firmly believed that he was climbing the ladder, and at the princely sum of £5 per condemned criminal, he would be providing much more for his family than in his work as a butcher.[8]

When the offer came along, Samuel did not need to give it too much thought. This was his ticket not only to provide financially for his family, but more importantly, he had finally reached his desired destination. Even though it would remain a secret for now, the times were changing with talk that he could remove his anonymity if he so wished and reveal himself before the Cestrian crowd in the future.

For Burrows, it was the prospect of removing his anonymity further down the line that sealed his decision. He knew that he could gain the much-needed attention that he craved but that he could remain anonymous if things turned sour as he was learning the ropes. He did not give it too much thought when he was offered the position.

At that precise moment in time, Burrows did not know about the consequences that lay around the corner. Like many jobs, he believed that it would be temporary yet bring some much-needed income into the home during desperate times. He never expected that he would be standing on top of New City Gaol for as long as he did, how the job would consume him, how his role would eventually destroy his family, or even how the job would nearly kill him.

Samuel Burrows was the city's new executioner but for now this information was only known by a select few. All he could do was wait for his first assignment but, with Harrison's new building completed, he knew it would not be long until he would be standing on its roof to complete his first execution.

Chapter 3

The Men Who Dropped Twice

William Proudlove and George Glover
New City Gaol, Chester, 1809

SAMUEL BURROWS COULDN'T sleep. The restlessness consumed him as he stared at the ceiling. He had planned for an early night so that he could be well-rested ahead of his first execution. He thought to himself that perhaps a drink would help him get some sleep. He turned to see Mary. She was already fast asleep as he gingerly made his way out of the bed. He knew every crack of the floorboards like the back of his hand so that even in the dark he could sneak around them. He gave Mary a gentle kiss on her cheek, put some clothes on, and quietly left.

Even though it was the late hours of the night, Northgate Street was still bustling with nocturnal activity. The inns and public houses were still a hive of commotion due to the vast amount of visitors who had arrived in the city earlier that day. Like Burrows, they couldn't sleep either. He ventured to the Dublin Packet on the Market Square of Northgate Street. He thought it would be quieter there compared to the northern section of the street. Once there, he found a seat and settled for a quiet nightcap.

Activity was still going on all around the city. The printers on Foregate Street and in Handbridge were working late into the night in order to finalise their broadsides that needed to be ready for the early morning. Hundreds of single, rough, paper sheets were hanging around their shops to ensure that the ink was thoroughly dry. An important and lucrative day awaited them as they knew that these single sheets of coarse paper would make them some serious money. With this in mind, it was all hands on deck as they wrote, printed, and published in haste. It had been a long wait for the printers to make such easy money. What they were currently working on would detail exactly why the events of the day were taking place. It would act as some sort of macabre memento for those wishing to purchase a grim souvenir of the day's action. After all, it was not every day that the city welcomed the event of a public execution.[1]

Over at the New City Gaol, the final preparations were being made at the scaffold, which was being constructed over its entrance. The building designed by Thomas Harrison had just opened and had already seen inmates moved from the old gaol at the Northgate.[2] To the prisoners, it would have felt like heaven when compared to the medieval gaol that they previously called home. Despite that, it was still a place no one really wanted to end up. The gaol contained those from the city, yet Chester had the luxury of having two gaols within its confines. As the final checks of the scaffold were made, those who had built it now headed to their beds.

The County Gaol was at Chester Castle. Chester was responsible not only for the punishments of those from the city but also for the county as a whole. Anyone facing trial within the county of Chester would find themselves here waiting for the biannual Assizes to hear their cases. Those sentenced to transportation to the colonies would be moved from the gaol after their conviction to hulks or other gaols. Those condemned to death would simply wait here until their date with the hangman. William Proudlove and George Glover were now spending their final night on Earth staring at their cell ceilings. Unlike Burrows, there would be no sneaking out. All they could do was wait.

When the morning came, Burrows was pacing around his Northgate Street home like a man possessed. Despite his lack of sleep, the excitement had taken its hold in ways he could not fully explain. Mary knew all too well that he sneaked out during the night as the smell of ale and gin escaped from his breath. As it lingered, she didn't mention anything. Now was not the time to wind him up. Instead, she prepared breakfast as she had done all her married life, only this time she sensed that Sammy was in elevated spirits. For him, the backbreaking days that he had spent as a butcher on the Shambles of Chester were now over. His new job as the city's executioner would bring in more money than they had ever seen before and if times ever got tough, he had plenty of skills that he could fall back on. She knew that the time had come for a decent payday, telling her two young boys Henry and Charles that soon they would be able to get some nice things.

Burrows had been one of the first in the city to witness the latest in executing technology as he was trained to use it only a few days prior. The 'drop' was the latest acquisition to complement the city's new gaol. It was a trapdoor mechanism where the executioner simply had to pull a lever in order to release the bolt that was maintaining a straight floor. Once the lever was pulled, the bolt would release, causing the trapdoor to open as the condemned plummeted to their inevitable deaths. It was designed to be a part of the scaffold so that after every execution, it could be safely stored away until called on again.[3]

As Burrows ate his breakfast, he kept repeating the process around his head. Place the condemned over the trapdoor, make sure the noose is attached correctly to the beam, and ensure that a strong rope is used and that the noose is made correctly. Tighten the noose around their necks and then pull the level to let gravity do the rest of the work. It all sounded so simple. What could possibly go wrong?

It had been a long time since the City of Chester last experienced the clamour of a public execution. Prior to the building of the New City Gaol, which was designed with the spectacle of execution in mind, condemned men and women were escorted from the County Gaol in Chester Castle or the dilapidated Northgate Gaol towards Gallows Hill in Boughton. It had been the place of execution for centuries and had witnessed its fair share and different methods used.

It was here where George Marsh was burned at the stake back in 1555 for heresy under the orders of Queen Mary I, but hanging was usually the preferred method of execution in Chester. Gallows Hill had ceased being used since the execution of John Clare in 1801. The unfortunate man pleaded his innocence and while being transported from the Castle to Gallows Hill turned his escape plan into action. Travelling along the River Dee on the back of a cart, he seized his opportunity, jumping off the cart with the aim of swimming across the river. The shackled Clare pulled off the first part of his spontaneous plan and made it to the river but in attempting to swim, the iron shackles weighed him down and slowly dragged him under to a watery grave. Undeterred, the hangman waded into the water to gather Clare's soaked corpse and proceeded to put his lifeless body back on to the cart and complete his journey to the gallows. Although dead, he was still hanged so the hangman could collect his pay.[4]

For the crowd that had gathered to witness the execution, it was an anticlimax. They expected to see a man struggle and fight for life until his final breath. To many, it was regarded as tasteless to hang a man who was already dead. Executions in the city later took place at the much-feared Northgate Gaol, but in Chester the idea of the spectacle of public executions turned sour. That was, until the completion of the New City Gaol.

The scaffold was designed to be placed on top of the gaol's entrance so that the crowds could now look up to see the convicts dangle high above them. Everyone could now get a vantage point and the execution became more of an event. It was also an opportunity for local businesses to set up crude takeaways among the jostling crowd with the aim of selling food and other such goods. The printers of Chester would also be around selling their freshly prepared broadsides to anyone who was interested in finding out more about the unfortunate souls about to be sent to meet their maker.

The New City Gaol's location was also pivotal, situated next to the new infirmary and just north of the Watergate where racegoers would enjoy the sport of kings at the Roodee racecourse. People could now enjoy the thunderous gallop of horses around the racecourse and the next day witness the commotion and hysteria of a public execution just a few hundred yards away.

Everything was happening around Samuel Burrows as he left his Northgate Street home for his new place of work. The Market Square was filling up as tired fishmongers, butchers, and grocers were beginning their new day by setting up their stalls. Burrows looked at the wooden shacks of the Shambles where he used to work.[5] He gave a nod to his former colleagues as he walked past, watching a new apprentice hack his way through the meat with a cleaver. Burrows remembered it all too well as he saw the congealed blood washed away into the cobbles of Northgate Street. There was no need for him to feel sentimental about what he was about to do. Death and butchery were all around him.

While he did not really need it, he felt that a dose of much-needed Dutch courage was in order. Even though Burrows gave the impression of a hardened man ready to take on anyone, he could not help but think about what he was about to do. Executing the men and thinking about the crime that they had committed did not even enter his mind. What was consuming him was the need to get it right. No mistakes, just get it done. A drink would steady those particular nerves. The Woolpack Inn on the Shoemaker's Row would see him regularly and today would be no exception.[6] A couple of drinks later, he would make his way towards his date with destiny.

The condemned men were still at the County Gaol at Chester Castle as Burrows was making his way through the streets. As he strolled down Watergate Street he could get his first glimpse of the crowds he would later entertain. William Proudlove and George Glover would soon come down this street as they were to be paraded through the centre of the city up Bridge Street before turning left down Watergate Street. The city was heaving as thousands made their way down to these streets, with many heading to up to the Rows for a clearer sight of the men as they slowly made their way down from one gaol to the next on the back of a horse-drawn cart that rocked along the cobbles. The crowds would then swiftly follow them down towards the gaol, with waves of people making their way down Watergate Street.

Samuel was on time; it was something that in his mind was non-negotiable. He loathed lateness in the same way that he loathed criminals. It was what impressed those who appointed him in the first place.

Burrows was a stickler for the law dating back to his days as the parish beadle for St Oswalds where he would perform his duties to the point of patrolling the area late at night searching for anyone causing a scene and then apprehending them before taking them to the holding house. In his mind, criminals needed to be punished, and now, as the city's executioner, he could do something that he believed was more important and rid the world of these unsavoury characters. No punishment was too severe and he was not scared to pull the lever. If anything, he was thriving at the opportunity to do so.

With his final checks completed, he looked up towards the beam that would be responsible for holding the weight of two condemned men. It looked strong enough but in reality it was impossible to tell. This might have been new ground for him personally but it was a new feat of engineering for the builders of the wooden gallows. His first assignment of prisoners had finally arrived at the gaol and they were now waiting in a holding room, where they were currently receiving their last rites. The crowd that had followed the procession from the Castle and the hundreds who had lined Bridge Street and Watergate Street had now massed outside the gaol. As they looked up they could see the gallows. It was nearly time.

William Proudlove and George Glover remained solemn as they awaited their execution. By all accounts, it was how they had been since their sentencing. The two men, aware that there would be no reprise for them, had behaved with nothing but penitence as they waited for the inevitable. They had both admitted their guilt for the robbery that they were a part of but continued to declare their innocence at shooting the officer of excise who had just so happened to be on duty at the time of the burglary. Either way, no matter who people believed, no one was fighting for a pardon.

The two men believed that the wounding of the excise officer was what led them to the gallows but in reality it was just a small part of it. Proudlove and Glover were part of a gang who intended to commit the armed robbery at the Lawton Salt Works just outside of Northwich. It was not the first time that the gang had descended on the Salt Works, and they had frequently plundered the area.[7] This time, however, they were detected by an excise officer. While Proudlove and Glover claimed that they did not fire at him, someone clearly did wound him and left him for dead.

It was only once Proudlove and Glover were caught that they identified the man who they claimed fired the shot. Robert Beech was the man they fingered for that crime and he was still at large. After they were found guilty by a jury, the judges at Chester Assizes sentenced the two men to death with the aim of it serving as a stern warning to any others who attempted anything similar. The two men had committed their crime at quite possibly the worst time in British history when it came to their eventual fate.

The Bloody Code was still in full swing within the kingdom. It allowed judges to hand out the ultimate sanction of the death sentence for over 220 crimes. The Waltham Black Act of 1723 may have been the legislation's official name but given its brutality, its colloquial nickname had firmly stuck. By 1809, many were now beginning to ask serious questions about the act and the methods in which the establishment was using it as a means to control the general populace. Prior to the passing of the act, around fifty crimes could see the perpetrator hanged, but over time more and more criminal acts were added to the statute books as the government was desperate to end all crime within the country. From murder, larceny, burglary, and forgery to more trivial crimes such as stealing from a rabbit warren, being out at night with a blackened face, poaching or even wrecking a fishpond; the risk of hanging from the executioner's noose was the highest it had ever been.[8]

The crime that saw Proudlove and Glover eventually hang was common throughout the county of Cheshire. Larceny and burglary were the most committed crimes in the county and took up nearly half of the cases that the Assizes would hear between 1760 and 1830. A crime against any form of property would lead to a higher conviction rate, with 64.5 per cent of all property-related burglaries leading to a conviction. Yet, Proudlove and Glover still had an opportunity to avoid the gallows.[9]

During the era of the Bloody Code, many who received the death sentence still managed to escape the hangman's noose. Between 1760 and 1830 a total of 571 criminals received the death sentence in the county and yet only 80 individuals were hanged in that time. The vast majority later had their punishments converted to sentences of transportation to Van Diemen's Land and Australia. Some 409 criminals from the county who had previously been sentenced to death had their punishments reprieved in favour of transportation. For Proudlove and Glover, there was such a possibility as they remained at the County Gaol at Chester Castle, but with each passing day the hope that they may have held on to was slowly slipping away.

Now, in their condemned cell at the New City Gaol after being moved from Chester Castle and paraded through the streets, any chance of a last-minute change of heart from the authorities had gone. Soon they would meet their executioner and the baying crowd who had waited seven years for a public execution, who were beginning to grow impatient.

No one in the crowd knew exactly who the executioner was and for now, Burrows liked it that way given that this was his first time on the gallows. That sense of anonymity would later become useful but given that this was his first execution, a combination of his jangling nerves and fear of reprisals somehow allowed him to focus on the job at hand. The gallows on top of the gaol had now been covered with black cloth in order to allow some dignity to Proudlove and Glover. What the crowd could see though was the trapdoor from which these men would soon descend. It was this black cloth that also meant that Burrows himself could hide himself from the masses. The days of the black hood covering the mysterious executioner were long gone in Chester now.

Burrows' first job was to pinion the men's hands behind their backs. He did this moments before they were due to be escorted from the condemned cell in order to prevent any calamity on the gallows itself. In some cases, executioners could face an ordeal when pinioning the condemned as they fought against the inevitable but Proudlove and Glover were in no mood to fight. Thankfully for Burrows, the depressed men had accepted their fate.

Burrows then climbed the wooden stairs with the condemned men, who were escorted by gaolers. Once there he placed a hood over the heads, took his slipknot noose, and then slid it over their heads before tightening it to their necks. The rope needed to be thick enough, depending on what Burrows believed their weight to be, and strong enough to ensure that it could maintain the hanging body for up to an hour after the condemned's final breaths. With the nooses attached to Proudlove and Glover, Burrows went over to his lever.

It all happened in a matter of seconds. The bolt was released as Burrows pulled the lever and the trapdoor opened. The gasps and cheers of the crowd filled the air as Burrows let out a sigh of relief. However, Burrows had miscalculated the weight of men and the thickness of the rope required. Soon the cheers turned into cries of abject horror as 'both ropes snapped a few inches from their necks, and the poor sufferers fell upon the terrace'.[10]

The sigh of relief Burrows previously exhaled had now quickly turned into panic as he looked up towards the beam where his ropes were attached. The beam was intact as his ropes billowed in the breeze. Unable to see exactly what was going on, he looked down the hole of the opened trapdoor to see his two condemned men lying metres beneath him in pain as their legs were covered in blood following their descent. Gaolers pounced on Proudlove and Glover and swiftly got them back to their feet before hastily taking them back into the gaol. They appeared 'to feel little either in body or mind from the shock that they had received'. Some of their vital functions had begun to shut down and, although nearly dead, they were not in 'absolute Death'.[11]

Once Proudlove and Glover had been revived they 'spoke of it as a disappointment' at still being alive, believing that they saw heaven.[12]

The two men requested that the gaol chaplain come and visited them again after being told in no uncertain terms that the execution was still going ahead. When Burrows heard the news he immediately went to find some more rope. This time though he picked the strongest around. Estimating weight and playing it by the book could wait until later; for now, he just needed to prove that he was the right man for the job. The drop was reset, the rope once again attached to the beam and after two hours Burrows had composed himself to go again.

Proudlove and Glover, despite the mishap on the gallows, remained calm. Perhaps there was a chance that their punishment could be converted to transportation after all? Maybe, just maybe, this was an act of god, who had somehow intervened in order to save them. They accepted the sacrament once again, while Burrows was frantically getting everything in place once more.

Burrows made doubly sure that the second time would go right. The crowd beneath him, he thought, were laughing as they continued to wait during the interlude. The whole process was then swiftly repeated. This time, it all went according to plan as Proudlove and Glover remained motionless moments after the drop.[13] There they waited lifelessly as the crowd finally dispersed and entered the inns and public houses of Chester to continue the assessment of what they had just witnessed.

Thankfully, no one was around when Burrows cut the men down. The post-execution stillness following the frantic events had exhausted him. He just hoped Mary hadn't seen him embarrass himself. Hopefully, she had stayed away from the Linenhall area but, given what had happened, Burrows was all too aware of the chatting lips that would eventually tell her everything they saw as they strolled down Northgate Street.

Placing the men's bodies on to a cart, Burrows enquired as to what happened next. He was told to go home, get himself sorted, and be ready for the next one whenever it may be. Somehow, he managed to keep his job. Burrows thought to himself that at least people would remember this one for years to come and at the very least they had no idea that he was the man who had messed it all up.

The Men Who Dropped Twice

As the cart left the New City Gaol it began its slow journey back to Odd Rode with Proudlove and Glover's lifeless bodies. A further punishment awaited them even in death. The two men were to be gibbeted near the Salt Works where their crime took place. Encased in an iron frame and raised above the highway for all to see, it served as a reminder as to what criminals could expect in the area when caught. While Burrows was enjoying his new-found riches, Proudlove and Glover's bodies were decaying in the gibbet as a warning to all.[14]

Chapter 4

A Done Deal

The Execution of Thomas Done
New City Gaol, Chester, 1810

NO MATTER HOW much Thomas Done pleaded his innocence it fell on deaf ears as far as Samuel Burrows was concerned. After all, for Burrows, it was nothing personal and the condemned man standing before him had been found guilty of murder. To Burrows, Done was just another job and this time he knew that he couldn't afford any mistakes.

Standing on top of New City Gaol, Done's execution was an opportunity to erase the memories of the men who dropped twice and Burrows knew he had to get this one right. He opted for thicker rope to ensure that it did not snap as Done plummeted. With the curtains closed, Burrows completed his checks as the masses gathered outside the gaol. Burrows could hear the murmurs from his vantage point as he carefully took a peek through the break of the curtains. While he was eager to reveal his identity as the city's hangman, he knew he had to bide his time, especially following the disaster of his previous effort. This one had to be perfect.

While Burrows' identity was still unknown, the same could not be said for Griffith Rowlands.[1] The surgeon was to be accompanied by Owen Titley at the Shire Hall as Rowlands prepared himself for an altogether different task. Not only was Done to be executed publicly but his body was also set to be publicly dissected by Rowlands. The stage was set with all the fixtures of a May extravaganza within the city. Not only was the execution of a condemned murderer set to get the crowds going but the city was also filled with racegoers eager to change their fortunes at the Roodee course.

A Done Deal

For the Corporation of Chester, May would become an important month for the city. The first race meeting of the season would ensure that the hotels and inns of Chester were full and the spectacle of a public execution merely generated more interest. Far away from Gallows Hill on the opposite side of the city, the New City Gaol was built just a stone's throw away from the racecourse. Now the public could easily move between both events as the crowds gathered in the same area.

Rowlands left his home on Abbey Street opposite Chester Cathedral and walked through Abbey Square. An eager Titley met him at his door as the two men walked together discussing the upcoming public dissection. To Titley, he was alongside a master of his profession. Rowlands had been a surgeon at the infirmary since 1785 and his wealth of experience was something that Titley admired greatly.[2] Soon, Titley would take over from Rowlands as Chester's lead surgeon responsible for dissection and anatomy.

The two men entered Northgate Street with the Exchange in full view as the crowds gathered around the fish and vegetable markets that filled the street. The commotion of the market filled the area with the vibrance of life as marketers peddled their wares, chanting their latest offerings to any who passed them by. Engrossed in his conversation, Titley ignored them, eager to hear about the proceedings that would follow Done's execution.

The corpse, Titley was informed, would be cut down by the executioner an hour after the condemned man's last struggle for life. This was to ensure that he was fully dead before he arrived at the Shire Hall. Then, and Rowlands even repeated it fully, they would cut down the chest, breaking the rib cage in order to remove the heart, which would be stored in a jar before the rest of the dissection could be completed. Rowlands encouraged his student to watch the procedure very carefully, in the same way that others would look at him when Rowlands eventually left the infirmary.

The two men strolled down Bridge Street, opting to use the Rows in order to keep away from the gathering crowds who were waiting for Thomas Done's procession to approach. Many were barging their way through in order to catch a glimpse of the condemned man as he passed through the streets on his way to date with Burrows' noose.

Rowlands was unimpressed with the whole charade. Here was a man of science who did not see his part in the events as a form of macabre entertainment for the masses. Looking around with an element of contempt at the crowds, he made his feelings clear to Titley that death was no theatre to be cheered for men like them, but at least it gave them an opportunity to explore the science of God's greatest creation.

The Shire Hall was empty when they arrived. Usually at times of the Assizes, the room would be filled with judges and barristers as the public galleries swelled with interest in the latest criminal cases. The two men looked around the emptiness of it all as they admired Thomas Harrison's architecture. Soon, the hall would be filled with crowds as they slowly walked down either side of Done's body as the anatomists carried out their work. With the body arriving once the hullabaloo of Done's execution was completed, the two men prepared their tools after they arrived with the rest of the team who were making their way from Chester Infirmary.

A few days earlier, Thomas Done stood in the dock before the Assize at the Shire Hall as he pleaded his innocence of the murder of Betty Eckersley. Done was not alone in the dock. Robert Holroyd was also facing the ultimate sanction as both men were the last people to see her alive.

Done and Holroyd were both flatmen working on the Bridgewater Canal that stretched from Runcorn to Manchester. It was while in Lymm that the two men encountered Betty and another woman while they were out drinking. Heading towards the canal, Done asked Betty if she would like to come on board his barge with him. It was an offer that she refused yet that did not appear to have deterred Done, who reportedly carried her away by force.[3]

The court heard more details of the men's alleged crime. Holroyd claimed that he left Done and Betty alone in order to prepare the horse that would later pull the barge along the footpath. Placing the horse in a nearby stable for the night, he returned to the public house, drank a pint of ale, and left at approximately eleven o'clock. Done and Betty were missing when he returned. Others were quick to confirm Holroyd's version of events and the Assize judges acquitted him quickly, leaving Done alone in the dock.

A Done Deal

The landlord of the nearby public house heard a commotion and the shrieks of a woman in distress. As he listened, he distinctly heard the words, 'O Lord Jesus'.[4] The landlord was not alone in hearing Betty's cries as more witnesses came forward to reconstruct the events of that night. Waking in the morning, the landlord began his day noticing that Done's horse and boat had vanished.

It was only days later that the body of Betty Eckersley was found. She was found in the canal just outside Lymm, tied up in a sack with her head still visible. Her neck was dislocated, with the brutal marks of violence found on her arms and breasts. It was estimated that nearly 60lb of weight had been tied around the sack in order to try and keep her body at the bottom of the canal. While the discovery of the body proved that Betty was indeed dead, it was still not enough evidence to condemn Done.

The key evidence came during the trial in Chester when a witness claimed to have seen Betty's body inside Done's barge the morning after her screams had pierced the canal-side calm. The witness could not distinguish if she was dead or merely asleep but it was enough to cause enough doubt as to her whereabouts the previous night. The evidence might have been circumstantial but Done made no defence to it.

Despite saying little during the trial itself, Done asserted his innocence as the judge was passing the death sentence. Done said to the court: 'I am innocent of the murder as your Lordship', before turning towards the jury in order to declare that he forgave them for their decision.[5]

Done's procession had left Chester Castle by the time that Rowlands and Titley had arrived at the Shire Hall. The Castle's vast open space in front of the Shire Hall still had some people hanging around as they slowly began to head to the New City Gaol. There were still a few hours to go until Done ascended the scaffold to face Samuel Burrows.

Burrows was prepared. He was a hive of activity behind the curtains that fluttered in the breeze. He had tested the mechanism a couple of times in order to ensure that the trapdoor opened fully and he visualised exactly where to place Thomas Done over the door. His thick noose was attached firmly to the crossbeam as he took a few breaths to calm himself down. Everything was going to be all right this time, he thought to himself.

Done was receiving his last rites as Burrows descended the stairs towards the holding room. Once the door was opened, Done stared at his executioner as Burrows approached him with rope ready to pinion the condemned man. Done proclaimed his innocence once more in a vain hope of catching some of Burrows' humanity. Sadly for Done, Burrows had a job to do and a family to feed. It was nothing personal; Done was going to hang and it would be faultless.

A sick feeling began to take hold of Done as he slowly climbed the scaffold. It was a nausea so intense that it forced him to faint as he climbed the stairs. Burrows took hold of the situation, grabbing Done and dragging him up the stairs before sitting him down over the trapdoor. With little time for games, Burrows shook Done until he woke before placing a hood over his head, standing the condemned man up and placing the noose around his neck.[6]

Burrows informed Done about the signal that was needed in order to alert him to pull on the lever. He gave Done a handkerchief and told him to drop it when he was ready. There was no need for a signal in Done's mind. He was about to die regardless. Defiantly, he dropped his handkerchief in front of Burrows as the two men shared their final conversation. Understanding the situation, Burrows nodded at Done before turning his back on him and descending down the steps towards his lever.

Burrows could hear the crowd. Their chants intensified as they knew that the time had finally come to see Done drop before them. There was a hushed silence as the crowd almost salivated with the satisfaction of what they were about to witness. Burrows closed his eyes and pulled. The cheers reverberated around the area. Burrows opened his eyes and looked at the taut rope on his crossbeam. It was still there. This time, he breathed a sigh of relief knowing that it had gone right.

The cheers could be heard across the small city as the inns of Chester prepared to swell. It was nearly their time to profit from Done's execution in the same way Burrows had as he collected his salary for his grisly work. Soon he would head for a drink but first he needed to cut down Thomas Done and then take him to the Shire Hall where Rowlands and Titley were waiting patiently for their cadaver.

With the May meeting at Chester Racecourse due to take place shortly, neither Rowlands nor Titley expected many to attend their public dissection of Done, although they still expected the morbidly curious to come to them rather than spectate the sport of kings. When Burrows arrived at the Shire Hall, he was in no mood to have a bit of chit-chat with the surgeons. Exhausted from his day's work, he simply wanted to head to the public houses of Chester to unwind. With his work now completed, it was now Rowlands' and Titley's time to complete their part of the execution.

The public dissection of condemned criminals was new to Chester. Previously murderers were placed in a metal gibbet as a warning to all but since the 1751 Murder Act, authorities were able to dissect the bodies of murderers in order to act as another punishment in a god-fearing society. The condemned criminal's body would be completely anatomised with only the skeleton, which could then be sold to anatomical schools or disposed of in other ways.[7]

Rowlands and Titley prepared the body and checked that Done was indeed dead by removing the heart. Then their meticulous study of the body could begin. Titley gave Rowlands an admiring glance. Standing before him was a man who had performed one of Europe's first surgeries on a broken hip and had previously removed a gallstone weighing 2¼oz, an operation that the patient, Thomas Jones, survived. Now, he was about to give a special lesson in anatomy not only to Titley but to the whole of Chester.

Chapter 5

Rage Against the Machines

The Executions of John Temples and Joseph Thompson
New City Gaol, Chester, 1812

THE GAOL AT Chester Castle had become almost full as forty-seven individuals entered between April and May 1812. As they filled the cells, they could hear the other prisoners and their sorrowful cries as they found themselves at the mercy of the courts.[1] The forty-seven were gathered quickly and placed into their new homes by Matthew Hudson and his gaolers. Hudson, the constable of the County Gaol in Chester, was slightly taken aback by just how many alleged Luddites were caught and it was now his responsibility to hold them until a special commission could be established.

Hudson now had seventy-one inmates within his gaol, with many inmates sharing cells designed for fewer people. For Hudson, it became a logistical nightmare to ensure that his prisoners were accommodated. The prison was built to receive approximately forty felons, with space for up to thirty debtors being housed in another part.[2] Overcrowding was nothing new for Hudson, who at certain times of the year saw his gaol swell with inmates. At one time, it was reported that around 200 prisoners occupied the gaol, either to carry out their sentence or await the Assizes.

Their reasons for being held at the gaol varied. During the spring of 1812, some were in custody awaiting trial at the ensuing Autumn Assizes due to take place later in the year, and this included John Lomas and Edith Morrey, who were awaiting trial for the murder of George Morrey, Edith's husband. Others, such as Richard Lewis and Samuel Shaw, were awaiting their trial for the highway robbery of William Gatley and Elizabeth Williamson.

Other prisoners such as Mary Walker were there for another reason. Walker was convicted at the Spring Assizes of 1809 for shoplifting. The 62-year-old had been incarcerated for over three years yet was lucky to even be alive. Originally sentenced to death, the courts reduced her sentence to transportation for life to Van Diemen's Land. Yet, mysteriously, she still languished under the custody of Hudson to become one of the gaol's longest-serving inmates.[3]

Michael Huntbach was also becoming a face all too familiar to the gaolers at Chester Castle. Sentenced at the Spring Assizes of 1807, the 74-year-old was also due to be transported. Instead, his seven-year sentence for 'refusing to deliver a schedule of his estate and effects to his creditors' meant that he dwelled in a debtor's cell, where he would remain until his debts were settled.[4]

James Lambeth was convicted of two indictments of assault in 1808.[5] As the hordes of new inmates arrived, he found himself away from them as he completed hard labour alongside six other men.[6] Lambeth would have known Samuel Burrows well enough to despise him. The hangman was becoming a regular fixture at the Castle. Under the terms of his retainer, Burrows was also called upon regularly to administer corporal punishment to inmates refusing orders. For those under sentence of hard labour, Burrows would use his authority to encourage them to work harder.

It was a role that Burrows was made for. He thrived on his authority even when he was a special constable for the City of Chester. Hardened and prepared to take any action that was necessary, Burrows was more happy to oblige. For the likes of Lambeth, the sight of Burrows filled them with as much dread as those about to face his noose.

Noticing the new inmates, Burrows got excited. He became eager to know more about them and what they had done. It had been a barren time for Burrows as in 1811 his noose remained still. Perhaps 1812 was his year?

✦ ✦ ✦

A perfect storm was brewing in the town of Stockport. Immigrants from Ireland had filled the town with the prospect of a better life and ample opportunities to work in the many factories. Offering cheaper labour, they quickly gained employment but the knock-on effect was catastrophic for the town as a whole. Swelling the population meant that those lucky enough to gain employment were doing so on lower wages, resulting in a massive decline in living standards and longer working hours. For the factory owners of Stockport, it was a straightforward case of supply and demand. With more workers available they could lower wages safely in the knowledge that any who objected could be easily replaced.[7]

For the Irish settlers, the situation that they had found themselves in was even more precarious. Unable to claim any form of parish poor relief, their position became even more desperate when factory owners installed steam looms and causing more unemployment in the area. Describing the area, the journal *The Philanthropist* highlighted that:

> Hundreds of families with three or four children have only ten or twelve shillings per week: such families cannot get sufficient food. A considerable number are out of work; others only partly employed; poor unable to buy clothes; in rags. Never before saw the labouring poor look so ill, or appearing so ragged; many miserably wretched; a few nearly in a starving state. Parish consists of 20,000, and the proportion of the inhabitants able to contribute is very small. The poor rate ten shillings in the pound on the assessment, and likely to be doubled, many who formerly paid being now obliged to apply to the workhouse for relief.[8]

It would not take long for tempers to fray as the desperate situation spilled into violence.

John Goodair was sitting comfortably at his home when the window was suddenly smashed. The window was shot through as eleven lead slugs were fired at his home, with him as the target of the attack. In a state of panic, Goodair called out for help and desperately checked on his family as he cowered on the floor to save himself from any further projectiles. Crawling on the floor, he could feel the glass scrape against his hands. Cutting himself as he crawled, he could hear the voices of those who attacked him. Fearing that they could enter the building, he crawled to the fireplace and reached for a poker in order to protect himself. Then, there was nothing.[9]

Sensing that his ordeal was over, he stood up gingerly, looked out on the street, and breathed a sigh of relief. Goodair, a factory owner in Stockport, was shaken but unhurt, for now. The attack was a warning from a group of Luddites who opposed the installation of new power looms that had seen many lose their jobs and others their pay plummet. Goodair's quest for profit and increased productivity was now a threat to his life. But if he believed that the situation was over then he, and many other factory owners in the north of England, would be sorely mistaken.

Incidents had erupted across the north, and in Stockport attacks on factories were becoming more frequent. William Radcliffe's factory and warehouse had already been attacked, during which a crowd of around 500 people smashed windows and threw in 5 torches in an attempt to burn the building to the ground. As the crowd quickly dispersed believing that the factory would burn, the alarm was raised. Radcliffe, who lived in a house adjoining his factory, rushed to save it and with the help of others was successful in doing so.

Aggrieved, Radcliffe was determined to find the culprits. The very next day, he issued a £200 reward to anyone who had any information that could lead to the capture of the ringleaders.[10] Given the situation and the promise of such a high reward, Radcliffe was hoping to not only to ensure the future safety of his own factory but also of others nearby. Yet no one came forward.

More attacks erupted across Stockport and the rest of the county. John Goodair, fearful of more serious threats to his life, decided to flee the town, leaving his wife and children behind. He did not make the choice lightly but he believed that with him out of the picture, he could indirectly protect his family from any further reprisals.

Tuesday, 12 April 1812 saw the rioting escalate with a fierce intensity. Around 3,000 weavers and loomers gathered and made their way to the mill owned by Thomas Garside. Arrogantly, Garside opted to talk to the crowd, who demanded a minimum wage. Soon the crowd turned nasty, throwing stones at the owner and threatening to kill him. Some in the crowd suggested that Garside was a government spy employed to find the ringleaders. Struggling through the crowd, Garside managed to escape the clutches of the mob and ran towards a cottage, where he was taken in. Fearful that the crowd might still find him, and for the safety of his good samaritan, he left only for the mob to find him once again. Baying for blood, the mob was determined to lynch Garside in the street until the leader raised his hand and told them to let the mill owner go.[11]

In Edgeley, a coordinated attack took place once again, this time outside John Goodair's warehouse. Without her husband to protect her, Mrs Goodair noticed the crowd and managed to flee with her children before they arrived at the family home. Fearing for their lives, the family fled, taking nothing with them. For the rioters, it was rich pickings as they raided the house, taking everything that they could. One of the thieves was later named as Joseph Thompson, who plundered what he could carry. He mainly targeted the silver collection, stealing 'one silver soup ladle, a quantity of silver spoons, and other articles the property of the said John Goodair'.[12]

Enriched by their raid of the Goodairs' home, Thompson and the others who were there on that fateful day set fire to it, burning everything within. Upon hearing about the destruction of her home, Mrs Goodair wrote:

> Everything, I have since learnt, was consumed by the fire, and nothing left but the shell. The mob next proceeded to the factory, where they broke the windows, destroyed the looms, and cut all the work which was in progress; and having finished

this mischief, they repeated the three cheers which they gave on seeing the flames first from our dwelling. It is now nine o'clock at night, and I learn the mob are more outrageous than ever ...[13]

Joseph Thompson was a forlorn figure as he stewed inside Chester Castle. It had been an ordeal not only for him but also for forty-seven other Luddites who were accused of breaking machines across the county of Cheshire. The only difference between him and the many others, was that he was sentenced to death for his involvement in the rioting. The forty-five individuals who appeared alongside him at the special commission that was held at the Shire Hall had all faced their own outcomes but alongside Thompson only one other man would face Samuel Burrows' noose.

John Temples had also been sentenced to death for his involvement in an incident in Adlington on 9 May 1812. The 27-year-old Irish weaver broke into the home of Samuel Wagstaffe with a gang of other Luddites and stole five silver teaspoons and a variety of other apparel. Both Temples and Thompson were punished not only for their involvement in the Luddite rioting but for the stealing of personal property. It was stealing more than the rioting that would eventually see both men attend the gallows at New City Gaol.[14]

For Burrows, it could have been an even more profitable session. Eleven Luddites were originally condemned to hang by the neck high above the Cestrian crowds but six of them were given the respite of transportation for life to Van Diemen's Land among other punishments. Burrows' disappointment at losing such a lucrative payday left him in a state of depression around Northgate Street as he ventured around the Shambles where he once proudly worked. For now, he was enjoying a kind of double life behind the veil of the anonymity of his new calling. Whenever asked why he looked so low, he simply gave out a slight smile and reassured his former colleagues that he was fine. But inside he was seething as more criminals slipped through his noose.

It would be an issue that would plague Burrows throughout his career. The courts would often reprieve those condemned to death, either through appeal or by opting for lesser sentences such as transportation. Each time it happened, Burrows felt as though he had personally been let down by a system that was meant to enrich him. But at least he still had two Luddites to execute as he prepared his rope. For now, though, he was busy thinking about what could have been and how it was taken away from him. Morals meant little to him when there was a small fortune to be made.

Richard Lowndes, William Greenhough, and John Heywood watched on from their cells as they saw John Temples and Joseph Thompson walk past them on their way to the Castle exit. The three men were desperately awaiting the outcome of their appeals against their death sentences but knew full well that the fate that awaited Temples and Thompson could soon be theirs to experience. Burrows had already seen six of the Luddites slip through his fingers and he was hoping that Greenhough, Heywood, and Lowndes would be his next payday soon after he had dispatched Temples and Thompson.[15]

Temples and Thompson left the Castle at half past twelve, where they were exchanged at the Gloverstone, Chester's natural boundary between the city itself and the county in which it lay, before being placed into a cart and paraded through the streets of Chester. Accompanied by a party of the Oxford Blues in order to ensure that no last-minute rescue attempts were made by other Luddites, security was tight across the parade route and thousands lined the streets to catch a glimpse of the condemned.[16]

Burrows was already eagerly waiting for them. It had been nearly two years since he last stepped up on the gallows of New City Gaol and he was itching to pull the lever that would send the two men into eternity. His mind wandered to thinking about where their souls would eventually end up. If God was forgiving then the gates of heaven could await them, yet Burrows believed that those who treaded his boards and felt the full wrath of the law were more than likely heading on the road to perdition for an eternity of punishment in the depths of hell. Samuel, although hardly a devout Christian, still believed in the moral compass of right and wrong. Yet the commandment of 'Thou shalt not kill', he believed, did not apply to him. Burrows did not see himself as a man who killed but as a man fulfilling the wishes of law and order. In his mind, when the Lord eventually judged him, it would be favourable. A necessary evil that is required to send condemned men toward their own eternal judgement. God's avenging angel for the people of Chester.

With the executions following Glover and Proudlove all being successful, Burrows began to feel a sense of arrogance about his work. The fear of failure had subsided and his identity was still largely unknown by the crowd beneath his feet. People were beginning to speculate as to the identity of Chester's hangman and around the public houses names were being highlighted. On occasions when he heard his name mentioned, he simply smirked and raised his eyebrows. While he was eager to tell people, he continued to hold back for the sake of Mary, Henry, and Charles. Yet it was an itch he simply could not wait to scratch. He was wondering just how much longer he could keep it a secret as he stood behind the curtain.

Despite being small in stature, Burrows still cut a menacing figure before those he was about to pinion. Standing 5ft 5in, he knew that some convicts could easily tower above him.[17] But Burrows was a hardened man. Years of butchery had seen him haul animal carcasses around and, although small in stature, he was full of fight. His aim was always to be two steps ahead of the condemned as he secured them tightly, anticipating any movements from them as they struggled. Most never put up a fight as he walked towards them, staring at them with his piercing grey eyes, and that was the way that he liked it.

The crowd saw Thompson struggle for nearly seven minutes as he slowly strangled to death. Burrows had placed the knot of the noose by the thick muscle of the neck away from the carotid artery. It would have been an agonising death that shocked the multitude of those who witnessed it. Temples, on the other hand, died almost instantly upon his fall. Burrows' error with Thompson's hanging created more of a spectacle in his mind, as he felt little empathy towards the men that died below him.[18]

Temples and Thompson hanged for an hour as the crowds slowly departed to continue the rest of their day. It was a sobering reminder of the full force of the law. This was the price that was to be paid by anyone who had the inclination to revolt. For the people of Chester still discussing potential acts of revolution, the hanging bodies of Temples and Thompson were enough to quell it. The authorities believed that their point had been made and the crowd's silence as the men dropped meant that the people had heard the ferocity of their warning.

For Burrows though, it was to prove to be a disappointing evening as he was later informed that Richard Lowndes, William Greenhough, and John Heywood were to be pardoned. The noose was once again replaced with the concept of transportation. Change was on the way but Burrows simply shrugged it off. Serious debates were emerging with regard to the death penalty, not just in Chester but in the country as a whole. It was a debate that threatened his very livelihood, his way of life, and also that of his young family.

Burrows browsed the newspapers with great interest following the execution of Temples and Thompson. While most simply restated the events that unfolded that particular day, some were beginning to become more critical of the practices on top of New City Gaol. The *Chester Chronicle* was particularly scathing in its assessment, stating:

> When men meet a violent death with such indifference, does it not strongly prove what we have frequently advanced, and which has been long our confirmed opinion, the inefficacy of taking human life. Surely some other punishment, more dreadful than death to the idle and the vicious, may be resorted to; and a thousand times more salutary in point of example to society.[19]

Needless to say, Burrows did not agree with them, especially when it came to murderers.

Chapter 6

A Very Public Ordeal

The Executions of John Lomas and Edith Morrey
New City Gaol, Chester, 1812 and 1813

SAMUEL BURROWS COULD hardly contain his excitement when the news came through. It was a case that caused a sensation throughout the papers, not only in Chester itself but across the whole county and even further afield. This would be the execution where everyone would finally know his name and with the double execution of John Lomas and Edith Morrey he knew that there would be little sympathy towards the condemned.

The prospect of executing a woman might have made many question their conscience but not every hangman had the same type of morality as Burrows. To him, Morrey was a murderer even though she did not commit the murder herself. Instead, he agreed with the local papers, who were busy claiming that she used her feminine powers to persuade her younger lover to murder her husband with the prospect of them running away together. In Burrows' mind, she had bewitched John Lomas, and that made her just as guilty as him.

Yet, the executions of Lomas and Morrey were far from straightforward affairs for Burrows. It would be a prolonged series of events that would see Burrows' work go beyond that of a simple hangman as he would also be responsible for the outcome of Morrey's still unborn child. But as Burrows prepared for the execution of her younger lover with only a few days' notice, he knew it would be a longer ordeal for Morrey.

How Edith Morrey came to stand before Burrows was the case of a classic Georgian scandal. A story of two lovers eager to start their new lives together. However, as with all stories that ended up at Burrows' scaffold, nothing was ever that simple. These two lovers had someone in their way, a problem that needed to be got rid of. That problem came in the form of Edith's husband, George Morrey.

George and Edith Morrey had been married for fourteen years before John Lomas had come on to the scene. By this point in their marriage, the couple had six children, although one had only survived for one year. While George was a successful farmer, Edith's eyes had begun to wander towards their younger farm hand, Lomas. It wouldn't take long before an affair between the pair began in the later months of 1811.[1]

With George frequently away on business, Edith and John's affair was becoming more serious. However, the couple's point of no return came when she discovered that she was pregnant with her younger lover's child. Now what began as a bit of fun became something much more murderous. What could they do? Well, they could always simply dispatch Edith's husband. After all, he was the only person standing in their way.

It was a rather simple plan. They would stage a break-in in which George would confront the burglar and become the unfortunate victim as he struggled with the assailant. The burglar would get away and in doing so leave the pair with no suspicions against them. What could possibly go wrong, they thought to themselves? With their plan now firmly rooted in their minds, all they needed to do was to kill George and get away with murder.

Hannah Evans slept with the Morrey children in the room adjoining the parlour. As a family servant, the couple knew exactly where she would be at the time they planned their crime. What they did not expect was for her to be a light sleeper who heard the blows to George Morrey's head and body.[2]

A startled Evans made her way to her window to open it. As she did the door opened. It was her mistress, Edith Morrey, whose face she could recognise from the dimly lit candle.

'You mustn't go out there, Hannah. I think there is a murderer in the house. What if he sees you?'[3]

The pair remained together with the children until the coast was clear. When all was quiet, Edith told Hannah to fetch John Lomas, who could alert the neighbours.

So far their plan was working exactly as they had intended.

With the neighbours gathered, including George's brother, they all went to Mr Morrey's bedroom on the ground floor to see the master of the house. George Morrey was found lying on the floor with his throat slit through his windpipe and damage to his left temple. Underneath his body was a blood-soaked axe. Edith Morrey told them about the break-in but upon closer inspection there was no evidence that anyone did so. The neighbours were now thinking that this was an inside job.

Soon suspicion rested firmly on John Lomas. What started as someone noticing a small area of blood on his wrist began to escalate as the neighbours inspected the area more closely. Soon they found blood in his room, and traces of blood leading from the stairs into his abode. Then came his clothing with blood stains on them. The neighbours called the constable. Lomas had nowhere to run.[4]

William Dooley, the parish constable, arrived on the scene alongside John Groom, who was a special constable and solicitor. Beginning their investigation, Groom questioned Edith Morrey, who was sticking to her story of a break-in. However, to the men of the law, something did not feel quite right.

Noticing the blood stains leading up to the room where Lomas lodged, they saw a small box. Could this be where the murder weapon was stored?

They then demanded that Lomas open the box he had kept in his room. Lomas was becoming difficult, arguing with the constables that it was his own personal property. Eventually, he conceded and led the police back to his room, only to find Edith already there. They were in time to see her take something from the box in an attempt to conceal it.[5]

While it was not a weapon that Edith was attempting to conceal, it was enough for the constable to take Lomas in for further questioning. Edith was trying to remove another blood-stained shirt. Lomas would go on to say that the blood was from a mare that had been taken to the blacksmith a week prior.

However, Lomas must have known that the game was up. Dooley took Lomas away from the scene and it was here where he made his extraordinary confession. Lomas confessed that he had in fact murdered George Morrey and then went on to implicate Edith as the principal figure in the killing, telling the constable that she had given him the signal to enter his master's bedroom when she was sure that George was asleep and handed him the axe.

Lomas would also go on to state that Edith was there when he killed her husband, holding the candle so he could see what he was doing. She even handed him the razor used to slit Morrey's throat when it became clear that he was still alive.

Heading back to the house to arrest Edith for her involvement following Lomas's confession, they allowed her time to get changed before escorting her away. It was at this moment that Edith attempted suicide by cutting her throat with a razor. Thankfully John Bellyse, a local surgeon, was there. She didn't cut herself deep enough and was swiftly patched up in order to await justice.[6]

Lomas was inconsolable with guilt, while Edith was still remaining steadfast with nerves of steel. The trial would see all of the main characters of this Georgian scandal in attendance. They wouldn't be alone. With the hysteria of this case sweeping the county of Cheshire and further afield, there was not a spare seat to be taken at Chester County Court.

Judge Robert Dallas and the jury had heard all they needed to hear during the four-hour-long trial as witnesses came forward to reveal what they knew about the night in question. The jury did not take long to reach their verdict; in fact, according to reports, they did not even need to retire.

Found guilty of the murder of George Morrey, Judge Robert Dallas sentenced them both to death by hanging at the New City Gaol. Even upon hearing the verdict, Edith remained calm.

In his summing up of the case, Judge Dallas said:

A Very Public Ordeal

As to you Lomas, I think it right to state that, although yours was the hand lifted up against the life of your master, and which affected his destruction with the dreadful axe first, and then the razor, yet you, we have every reason to believe, are the least guilty offender of the two; for it cannot be doubted that in the hardened heart of another was lodged that malice which hatched the plan to execute, through your means, so foul a murder – and I grieve to add, you were but too easily seduced.[7]

In the eyes of Judge Dallas, it was Edith Morrey who was the mastermind of this murder, using her besotted lover to fulfil the deed. For the murder of George Morrey, the judge could only hand one sentence to John Lomas. He was to be executed. For her part in this murderous affair, Edith Morrey was also condemned to die. There was, of course, a divide of opinion as the gasps rang out in the courtroom.

Riddled with guilt, Lomas dramatically cried out. In his mind, he deserved the punishment that was coming his way. Edith, on the other hand, was fully expecting to survive. Despite Lomas's cries, Edith said nothing and instructed John Cross to inform the court that she was pregnant, and for this reason she could not be executed at this time.

Edith was right; given her circumstances, she could not be executed, at least until after the child was born. She was removed from court to the home of Matthew Hudson, the governor of the County Gaol at Chester Castle, where she was to be examined by a panel of matrons who would confirm that she was 'quick with child'. In other words, she was approximately five months' pregnant.[8]

For Morrey, her pregnancy would provide her with a stay of execution. She would, of course, have been hoping that opinions might change and that she could get off with a more lenient sentence. She had time to at least try to save her life, but Lomas didn't.

There was not much time for Burrows to prepare. With the death warrant signed, Judge Dallas ordered that the execution should take place just two days after his sentencing. Yet if Burrows did not have much time, then it was even more rushed for those looking to profit. With only two days' notice, the scaffold was already being prepared above the entrance of New City Gaol. While everything was slowly getting into place, Burrows was feeling extremely eager to pull the lever once more.

On the morning of 24 August 1812, John Lomas awoke for the final time. He had spent the weekend preparing for his inevitable fate at the hands of Burrows. In a letter to his father, he told him of his love for him and his sisters, urging them to pay him one final, sorrowful visit.[9] Meetings were high on Lomas's agenda. He had asked the governor of Chester Castle, Matthew Hudson, if it would be at all possible to talk with Edith. Hudson dutifully agreed.

The two lovers sat together, with Lomas asking her for her forgiveness. At first, Edith said little as Lomas continued to apologise for pointing the finger at her during his confession. Then Edith finally responded in one final act of reconciliation between the two. She said, 'I have forgiven everybody and everything that has been done against me.'[10]

For Lomas, it was enough to satisfy him as he embarked towards his terrible ordeal.

On the morning of his execution, Lomas felt that he had done as much as he could have possibly done in order to satisfy himself. He knew that once he departed the Earth, he at least had some form of forgiveness from Edith. Before his impending parade through the streets of Chester, Matthew Hudson instructed his deputy, George Hurst, to take Lomas on a brief tour of the five wards of Chester Castle to say his goodbyes.

Hannah Holland shared her sleeping quarters with Edith Morrey. Lomas approached but Edith could not face him for that one final farewell. Speaking to Hannah on the other side of the door, a tearful Lomas begged Holland to give Edith a message.

'Tell my mistress not to forget her prayers and Bible. I shall be in heaven soon.'[11]

It was an unmistakable sound that could be heard on the cobbled streets of Chester as Teddy Bock ventured around the crowds eagerly awaiting the parade of John Lomas. Bock only had one leg that was his own, the other was fashioned from wood.[12] Each step was followed by the clanking sound of his wooden leg against the firm stone cobbles. Everyone knew when Teddy was around as the tobacco from his pipe filled his surroundings. Soon he would begin to sing, with his deep baritone voice penetrating the silence of the crowd.

The song he was about to sing was a mournful tune that he had cried out so frequently. With some copies of his sorrowful lyrics in his hand, he hoped that some with the crowd would buy it off him. As Lomas's carriage slowly arrived up Bridge Street, Bock released his latest ballad:

> Good people all I pray attend,
> Unto these lines which here is penned;
> A cruel murder I did commit,
> And now I do repent of it.[13]

For the masses who surrounded Teddy Bock that morning, the full story of Lomas and Morrey's actions that fateful evening in Hankelow was sung out aloud to them. With Lomas's carriage drawing ever closer, Bock timed his ballad to hit optimum impact as those around him finally saw Lomas looking away from the crowd.

Bock sang:

> My mistress by me she did stand,
> All with a razor in her hand,
> 'Take this', she says 'and end his life
> And I will be your loving wife.'[14]

Lomas had heard Bock's gruesome tune but chose to ignore it. It had made those around Bock even more vengeful towards Edith. Yet, she was nowhere to be seen as Lomas continued his journey toward Burrows and his noose. As the carriage passed, Bock and hundreds of other fellow Cestrians followed, making their way to New City Gaol as he repeated the verses of his song.

Bock gathered more attentive ears as his booming baritone filled the streets of Watergate Street before turning right at the Watergate itself. The gates of New City Gaol opened to let Lomas's carriage in before swiftly closing once the condemned man was inside. The masses continued to gather as Bock continued to sing, hawking copies of his lamination to the hordes that surrounded him. There was plenty of competition around Bock as the broadside sellers moved around the crowd selling their single-sided sheets full of gruesome details. Food sellers were also meandering among the masses offering snacks to all who required sustenance. The carnivalesque atmosphere was in full swing as they waited patiently.

Finally, Lomas revealed himself high above New City Gaol. The black curtains that surrounded the gallows quivered as he stood in front of the masses. Suddenly there was silence as the condemned man was about to speak. Teddy Bock hushed mid-verse as the crowd waited to hear what Lomas had to say. Then, he said what would be his final words: 'Gentleman, take warning by my fate: avoid evil actions – and may the Lord Jesus Christ have mercy on all your souls.'[15]

Lomas turned and went back through the curtains as Samuel Burrows placed him over the trapdoor. Placing a hood over Lomas's head, he then guided his head through the noose and attached it around his neck. The crowd remained still, each eagerly awaiting the drop. While much could not be seen, the crowd focused their attention on the bottom of the trapdoor, watching the bolt intently. Burrows waited for his signal and then pulled the lever.

Lomas plummeted and the masses erupted in cheers as his body fell. Those hawking their macabre merchandise went into overdrive as the crowds slowly began to depart toward the nearby inns in order to gossip more about the unfortunate Lomas. In the meantime though, as Lomas's dead body swung in the summer's breeze, there was still work to be done.

As the cheers reverberated around the gallows at the New City Gaol as John Lomas dropped, Dr Owen Titley was busy getting himself prepared. He knew he had about an hour until his work could officially begin. As Burrows goaded the crowd for more applause, Titley and his assistant were making their final checks on their equipment. It wouldn't be much longer until Lomas was coming to them. The 32-year-old surgeon was responsible for the very final act of Lomas's punishment. That was that his body was to be dissected and publicly anatomised.

The death warrants of both John Lomas and Edith Morrey named Dr Titley as the man responsible for their public dissection.[16] It was a moment in his life that he felt he was more than prepared for following his apprenticeship under Griffith Rowlands. During the anatomisation of Thomas Done, Titley had observed meticulously the methods of Rowlands but with the good doctor now elsewhere there was no one to turn to should things go wrong. Soon it would be his time to become the master as others watched him at work. While he was nervous, there was also an element of excitement in his pace as he gathered his tools.

Anatomy and the advancement of medical knowledge was becoming an industry in Georgian Britain. While Edinburgh and London would become the key focal points of anatomical advancement within the kingdom, areas such as Chester still played their own pivotal roles.

There was, of course, a key issue when it came to the desire for knowledge. Bodies for anatomical research were in short supply. Condemned murderers and suicides were permitted to be used for research, and at times paupers or those who died in the street. However, this was only on the condition that the deceased were not claimed by families within forty-eight hours.

This lack of bodies compared to the demand by anatomists was one of the key reasons for the rise of the resurrectionists, the collective term used for those who went out of their way to steal recently consecrated bodies. The resurrectionists would look for freshly dug graves in order to steal the bodies from the ground. Then they would sell them to anatomists in order to further their research and enrich themselves.

This caused concern, not only among the government but also those who were laying their loved ones to rest. For those who could afford it, mortsafes were installed over the grave in order to make it harder for the resurrectionists to steal the body. These metal grilles can still be seen in a number of cemeteries, especially in Edinburgh.

It was in the epicentre of medical research where William Burke and William Hare would thrive. The only difference between them and the resurrectionists that surrounded them was that Burke and Hare were able to provide Doctor Knox with even fresher bodies. The reason for this was that they were not digging up bodies. Instead, they killed in order to meet the demand. The West Point murders were a key reason for a change in the law.[17]

However, Chester was not a hub for anatomical research. Instead, Owen Titley performed the dissection as part of the punishment for murderers. The trial of the two lovers would be the only occasion that he conducted dissections in conjunction with the Murder Act of 1751. As Titley watched out of the window of the infirmary next door to the New City Gaol, he knew that time was already against him.

Judge Dallas had ordered that Lomas should endure a two-day public anatomisation but the heat of the August summer's day was already creating an issue for the surgeon. Burrows' insistence that Lomas should hang for a further hour just like anyone else had meant that the body was already in the early stages of composition. Titley knew that a two-day anatomisation was out of the question.

Burrows cut down Lomas on the hour and took the body next door to the infirmary, where Dr Titley was waiting impatiently for him. Burrows handed Lomas over, dusted his hands, and then quickly departed to the alehouses of nearby Watergate Street.

A Very Public Ordeal

There would be little rest for Dr Titley. Instead of moving Lomas to the Shire Hall for public dissection, he went against the orders of the judge and performed the anatomy in the infirmary. Time was already against him as he made his first incision. He opened up the thorax and abdomen, removing the heart in haste. While he should have then sewed up the body and sent it to the Shire Hall, he continued with the rest of the anatomisation, rendering it down as quickly as he could. At eleven o'clock the next morning, members of the Chester Infirmary's management board held a meeting and learned that Titley had completed his work. They were told that 'the bones of Lomas the murderer' were ready to be dispatched to London.[18]

An unborn child had saved Edith Morrey from Burrows' noose the day her lover fell from the gallows but even she must have known that it could not save her forever. She was still hoping for a stay of execution but as time passed she knew that hope was fading. She languished in her cell at Chester Castle now heavily pregnant and by December she had spent nearly four months there. Doctors visited her regularly as the time to give birth quickly approached.

Morrey's contractions began in the later hours of Sunday, 20 December as nurses attended Edith in her cell. Knowing that it would not be long until the baby was born, she was comforted but still remained in her cell as her screams reverberated around the Castle. In the early hours of Monday, she had given birth to a young boy, who she named Thomas Morrey. Yet she would not spend much time with her newborn son as arrangements were being made to remove him from his mother into the care of William and Edith Coomer.[19]

The law clearly stated that women who gave birth under the threat of execution were to be given one month's grace before arrangements could be carried out. Knowing that she had some time, Edith continued to maintain her innocence and begged for a pardon. Her stay of execution was further prolonged until April, when the Spring Assizes gathered in 1813. This time, a new death warrant was issued. Despite her long stay at the Castle and her continued attempts to gain a reprieve, the execution of Edith Morrey would still take place.

As preparations for Morrey's execution commenced, Burrows was informed that the black curtains that he was becoming so used to were to be taken down by the Chester Corporation for the execution in order for the public to be able to see the full horror of an execution.

For so long Burrows had enjoyed a level of anonymity as he pulled the lever that sent the condemned into the eternity that awaited them. It did not bother him either way as he had sometimes been prone to reveal while drunk his grizzly profession following the execution of John Lomas. Glimpses of Burrows were often seen as the curtains were disturbed by the breeze but now they could all finally see him in all his glory. It was an anonymity that had always been designed to prevent any repercussions for the man who held the post of the city executioner and on the whole it had worked for centuries. Hangmen were far from popular within the community but Burrows had always felt the urge to showboat. Now he was finally given his opportunity to put on his show.

It was reported that 10,000 people gathered around the New City Gaol to witness Morrey's final moments. Burrows was used to large crowds but even he had never seen an audience of this size before. When he revealed himself to the masses beneath him, he did so with the manner of a ringmaster who revealed in the cruel theatre of it all. With his arms raised, he taunted the crowd, who lapped up every second. This was now Burrows' stage and for this moment he was the centre of his own universe.

He was already slightly drunk by the time he trod the boards of his gallows. His new set piece was to play to the crowd and attempt to balance on a stool as he lassoed the noose over the timber crossbar. After a few attempts, he finally succeeded as the masses cheered. To those who loved to witness a public execution, Burrows was their new darling. He aimed for the lowest common denominator with his own take on gruesome theatre. This was low-taste entertainment at its finest.[20] Yet for those who loathed this kind of theatre, Burrows represented all that they hated. A drunken, brutal, and loathsome character who took pride in the knowledge that he was about to send someone to their death. Burrows cared nothing for the naysayers. Instead, his focus was firmly on those who cheered his every move.

As Morrey ascended the gallows, the crowd's cheers were quickly replaced by respectful silence. With her hands still free, she approached Burrows so that he could pin her wrists together. In order to maintain her dignity, Burrows then fastened rope around her ankles in order to prevent her legs from kicking. Throughout the whole scene, Morrey remained dignified, almost fearless about her fate.

Morrey remained silent on the scaffold. Burrows then placed a handkerchief between her fingers and told her to let it go when she was ready to depart the Earth. The crowd waited with bated breath in the hope that she would say something to them. Burrows asked her if she wanted to say anything before he put a white hood over her head. Remaining defiantly silent, Burrows took the hint and placed her head in the hood before guiding her to the trapdoor and placing the noose around her neck.[21]

The mood had changed from one of Burrows' attempts at dark comedy to sorrowful respect. With Morrey in full show to the Cestrian crowd, Burrows descended the scaffold to approach his lever. He waited for his signal and pulled, releasing the bolt from under Morrey, who fell in microseconds.

For two and a half minutes, Morrey jerked and spasmed in front of the crowd until she remained still as her lifeless body swayed in the breeze. Burrows watched his crowd depart the Linenhall area and waited a customary hour before cutting Edith down.

Edith Morrey's lifeless body lay in front of Dr Titley. Unlike John Lomas, he knew he could not perform the dissection entirely in private. What he did previously had caused him much grief from the authorities, who this time insisted that Morrey be taken to the Shire Hall where the public could witness her dissection. He made the same cuts that he had made to Lomas and removed her heart before sewing up her body. Burrows waited and watched the surgeon as he did so. After all, someone needed to make sure that her body got to the Shire Hall.

Burrows watched on with a morbid interest as Dr Titley removed Morrey's heart. It reminded him of his days working in the Shambles when he was a butcher. As he saw the blood flow from every incision, Dr Titley thought that perhaps Burrows might squirm in the way many others had before. Yet, Burrows remained steadfast and completely unmoved, recalling tales from his time in his previous profession to the good doctor. With Dr Titley finishing up his final stitches, Burrows began to grow impatient. He wanted to get it done as quickly as he could so he could swing by the Golden Eagle on his way home.

Morrey was placed carefully on to a cart before the hangman took on the weight of both handles and slowly made his way up Nuns Road towards the Castle. Although short in distance, it was still a long trudge for Burrows. Each step sapped his energy further as the weight of the cart weighed heavily on his shoulders. He could not stop thinking about the crowd that saw him in action. It was the largest he had ever seen before and he was pleased with the show that he had put on for them. That was the part he loved more than anything. The laughter as he stumbled on the gallows, the revulsion on their faces as he mimicked being hanged himself, and the roars of excitement as he finally pulled on the lever sending the condemned to meet their maker. But this was the part that few saw as he painfully delivered the cadaver back to the Castle. He stopped for a moment to wipe the sweat from his brow with the Castle in his view. Next to it, the Golden Eagle was Burrows' main priority, where he knew that he could quench his thirst. He only had a few more agonising steps until his reward awaited him.

✦ ✦ ✦

A Very Public Ordeal

Edith Morrey's body was swabbed in formalin and remained in the Shire Hall overnight. She was watched overnight as more formalin was applied to her at regular intervals in order to preserve her body. The smell of formalin filled the hall, making the eyes of those preserving the body water constantly. With his work complete, Burrows did not attend the public dissection performed the next day by Dr Titley. Instead, he opted to make use of his day in the alehouses of Northgate Street. It was an eerie feeling as Burrows made his way around the street. Northgate Street was all but deserted as thousands of people headed to the Castle. Once there the masses would gather, chatting about the previous day's execution and continuing to gossip about the crimes of Lomas and Morrey.

The crowd would then slowly enter the Shire Hall in line, walking around the corpse of Edith Morrey on either side in order to catch a glimpse of Dr Titley in action. His main concern was not the passing crowd but his students, who were watching him dissect for the purposes of anatomical knowledge. To the crowd, it was merely another chance to tell people that they were there to witness Morrey's ordeal even in death. But to Dr Titley and his students this was serious science in action.

The crowd could see each organ slowly being removed from the cadaver and then carefully placed into jars containing alcohol. Dr Titley was acting slowly, making the most of each incision that cut the body of Morrey. This part of the procedure was, however, a token affair; one for the crowds more than for the students themselves. They were there to keep everything official as approximately 10,000 people strolled past the body of Edith Morrey.[22] This was anatomy as spectacle rather than science, and Dr Titley knew it. The charade lasted until the final spectator left the hall. Appeasing the authorities of the city, Dr Titley packed up his equipment and almost lovingly placed the body back on to a carriage. The rest of the anatomisation would be conducted in private between himself and his students back at the infirmary. Edith Morrey's very public ordeal was now over.

Chapter 7

The Tragedy of Miss Porter

The Executions of William Burgess,
James Yarwood and William Wilkinson
New City Gaol, Chester, 1813

LIKE MANY IN the local area, Mary Porter made her way to Chester in an attempt to gain employment and to start a new life. It had worked for the likes of Samuel Burrows, who left the village of Ravensmoor. While he succeeded by entering the Shambles of Northgate Street as a butcher, many would eventually leave Chester as the city faced a steady decline. Like most formerly previously prosperous places, Chester also fell victim to the rise of industrialisation. Its once busy ports were slowly becoming a shadow of their former selves as the River Dee silted and industries moved away in favour of the emerging industrial metropolises of Liverpool and Manchester. That is not to say that Chester was not booming in some areas. There were still plenty of opportunities within the city with retail businesses growing as well as the new leadworks, which proved to be vital employers. However, the recent swell of arrivals saw the city grow to a population of 16,140 in 1811, and its lack of industrial opportunities meant that not all were successful.[1]

Originally from St Helens, Mary Porter had found herself almost destitute like the daughters of so many weavers in the area. The rise of industrialisation and the immense growth of the factories was wiping out the more traditional cottage industry of weavers throughout the north of England. A once proud tradition where employment was plentiful had become a struggling trade in which Mary and her family had become yet another victim of the rise of the machines.

Her father, John Porter, had reached the point where sustaining his daughter financially had become too much, and with work growing hard to find, Mary left her family home in order to attempt to gain work as a domestic servant in Chester. She began her brief time in the city with Peggy Cuncliffe, who was a relative. Despite her attempts to work, she failed. Dejected by her constant rejections, she felt that it was the right time to return home and try to find something else. It would be a decision that would have dire consequences.[2]

Leaving Chester behind, a cold and vulnerable Mary embarked on the long walk home. Tired, hungry, and in need of the quickest possible route home, she approached a stranger in the town of Frodsham who advised her to get the ferry from Weston Point over towards Runcorn and from there take the road to St Helens. Taking the stranger's advice, she continued on to Weston Point.

Noticing a small hut on the Weston Point, Mary enquired about possible departure times. William Wilkinson opened the door to her. Standing at imposing 6ft tall with broad shoulders, Wilkinson advised her to speak to his friends, who knew the ferry better than him. He pointed her in the direction of William Burgess, who claimed there was little chance of the ferry leaving soon due to the low tide but he offered to keep her company until the time was right. Taking her to a nearby inn, the pair waited.[3]

William Wilkinson and James Yarwood entered the inn soon after and the four of them drank until it was nearly time for Mary to continue her journey. Fearful of the night-time crossing, Wilkinson offered Mary a place to stay for the evening. Against her better judgement, she agreed. It was on the walk from the public house to Wilkinson's home that Mary was brutally attacked.

The rape of Mary Porter was considered so brutal that the full details of the crime were never printed in full, much to the public's annoyance. Describing the perpetrators as 'inhuman monsters', the press was also keen to highlight Mary as conducting her evidence at trial with 'the greatest of propriety'. This was despite her ill health following her ordeal, causing her to remain seated while giving evidence for nearly three hours.[4]

The jury declared the men guilty but recommended that mercy should be shown for their lives. Judge Dallas, however, disagreed with their request for mercy, suggesting that 'he was fearful it could not be granted'. Mr Cross, who was defending the three men, again asked for leniency but Judge Dallas overruled once again and set their execution of 29 May 1813.[5]

With a triple execution planned, Burrows was in a vibrant and playful mood. Even Mary was slightly taken aback as he planted multiple kisses on her cheek in a tender manner. Following the execution of Edith Morrey, Burrows was in for a bumper year with a total of four executions. That total would rise to seven with another triple execution taking place later in the year, but for now he had already reached a new record.[6] Times were good within the Burrows household in terms of their finances at least.

Even though Burrows was riding high in terms of his finances, the same could not be said about how he was being perceived in the streets of Chester. His previous antics on the gallows were considered to be in poor taste as he attempted to lasso his noose over the supporting beam while clearly intoxicated. For Burrows, he considered this to be a part of the service he provided. He saw himself as part executioner and part showman; a morbid entertainer whom most of the crowd enjoyed watching. But the opinion of him in the local press was much more negative. To the authorities who had hired him, Burrows was beginning to become a liability for his drunken antics, and they were already preparing to keep an eye on him in case he ever turned up on the gallows in a drunken state again.

They opted to tell Burrows about what would happen if he ever did it again. If he was drunk the night before the execution, he would be taken to the New City Gaol swiftly and placed in a cell in order to sleep it off so he could have a clear head for his actual work. Burrows agreed with the idea, or at least he did at that particular moment in time. Some members of the council were disgusted with this but it was easier to keep Burrows than to completely dismiss him and search for a new hangman. Either way, Burrows had somehow managed to keep his job.

The nature of the crime committed by William Wilkinson, James Yarwood, and William Burgess repulsed the city and the authorities. It was one of the few times that they were glad to have a brute like Burrows as their man on their gallows. What repulsed them further was the men's behaviour in the Castle gaol, which was described as 'highly reprehensible and indecent'. Burrows had also taken a dislike to his next victims. Given what he had read in the local papers, these three men represented everything he stood against. Unlike his feelings towards executing Edith Morrey, on this particular occasion the day could not come soon enough for him.[7]

On the night before their execution, all three men were given the customary sermon by the gaol's chaplain. Knowing that their end was near and with the realisation of what was happening, both Yarwood and Burgess began to feel remorse for what they had done. Yarwood in particular felt the moment with force, breaking down in tears throughout the sermon. Wilkinson, on the other hand, remained steadfast and showing no signs of being moved in any way.

Burrows would have missed the commotion of the three men's procession through the streets of Chester. While he was busy tending to the gallows on the roof of New City Gaol, the convicted men embarked on their journey down Bridge Street. The ballad mongers were in full force alongside the broadside sellers clambering to sell their merchandise as the streets were lined with those wanting a glimpse of the condemned men. Riding in a cart along the cobbled streets, the three men continued with their meaningless bravado. Wilkinson saw some old friends standing on the corner of Bridge Street and Watergate Street as the procession turned left. He shouted in their direction: 'Never mind my lads! Keep up your spirits – we are all of us murdered men! But never heed, I'm just as happy as if I was going to a play!'[8]

If the people of Chester were expecting any form of remorse and a plea for forgiveness from Wilkinson then they were to be disappointed. His particular antics would continue on the gallows, much to Burrows' personal annoyance. Wilkinson continued to shout as Burrows placed the noose around his neck. After upstaging the executioner, Burrows made sure he strung him up tightly, if anything in an attempt to shut him up. But Wilkinson continued regardless, shouting to any who would listen that this was all a set-up and that his new handkerchief 'fits me nice and tight'.[9]

The other two men's bravado had ceased. The magnitude of what faced them had finally set in. Burrows placed the black hood over their heads and walked towards his lever, giving it a gentle stroke before gripping it firmly. He could hear the anxiety coming from all three as finally Wilkinson stopped shouting.[10] It was this silence that Burrows enjoyed the most each time he prepared to pull his lever as a gentle wind swirled around him. The crowd below him remained still, waiting to see the condemned drop. The silence would only last a matter of seconds before the crowd would erupt once again. In Burrows' mind, this was the equivalent to the rapturous applause that those who graced the theatres must have experienced. He waited a little bit longer and then pulled.

The trapdoor opened, sending all three men down. Wilkinson died almost instantly. Burgess was also swiftly dispatched but Yarwood suffered, fighting against the force, and slowly strangled high above the Cestrian crowd for nearly four minutes. Burrows, unmoved, watched intently as Yarwood struggled. The crowd might have expected the hangman to use Yarwood's struggle to help whip up a further frenzy, but instead, he just watched unemotionally as the man fought for his life.[11]

With an hour to wait until he could eventually cut the three men down, Burrows turned to his superiors and told them that he was going for a drink. On this occasion they agreed with Burrows; after all he had managed to do complete his task sober so in their eyes progress was being made. Burrows headed up the incline towards Watergate Street in order to pay the Old Custom House Inn a visit. It was here where he frequently visited after executions for a drink. The regulars noticed him and asked him why he seemed so subdued on the gallows compared to previous events. Burrows ranted about his recent orders to remain sober on the gallows as others began to laugh around him. They knew it couldn't possibly last, and so did Burrows.

Chapter 8

This Time It's Personal

The Execution of William Wilson
New City Gaol, Chester, 1814

THE NAMES OF the convicted meant little to Samuel Burrows. To him, they were just another criminal waiting to be hanged. However, the case of William Wilson would somehow have felt more personal to him. He might not have remembered his name following their brief encounter but his face would have undoubtedly been etched firmly into his memory.

Wilson knew exactly who his executioner was as he climbed the steps towards the gallows. He thought that for Burrows there could have been an element of revenge waiting for him.[1] Questions must have swirled around his head as he slowly ascended the steps towards his eventual destiny. If Burrows did indeed recognise him, would he go out of his way to make it as slow and agonising death as he possibly could? Or with their encounter being nearly a decade prior, had Burrows forgotten what he looked like? Wilson was hoping for the latter.

Their brief encounter came during a different era of Burrows' life. In 1804, Burrows was not the hardened man that he was to become. Back then, he was a much more respected figure within Cestrian circles. He worked as a butcher in the Northgate Street Shambles and while it was hard, physical work, Burrows did not mind. He had firmly established himself within his new city. His son, Henry, was entering his third year and by all accounts Burrows was happy. Fatherhood was treating him well and his relationship with Mary was one of optimism. Within the city itself, he was also becoming a well-known figure due to his work as a parish beadle.

It was a position that deeply appealed to a man like Burrows. He believed in the law of the land and was more than capable of fulfilling the duties that came with the position. As a beadle, Burrows was responsible for most of the order within the parish of St Oswalds in the centre of Chester. His main duties were to ensure that churchgoers arrived on time and were attentive at Sunday gatherings. It was also his responsibility to ensure that the children of the parish were attending Sunday school. Any misdemeanours from any party would be punished by his hands. Yet church was not his only duty. He would also act as the parish's law and order, resolving neighbourhood squabbles, escorting troublemakers to the watch-house, and patrolling the area regularly. For a man like Burrows, it gave him the status he desperately craved.

Burrows had been assaulted before during his duties. If anything, it was part of the territory. He had managed to merge his duties as the parish beadle with his other role as a special constable. Perhaps he took his role too seriously, making altercations more frequent. In 1801 he had previously been assaulted by Joseph Ridgeway while carrying out his duties but trouble was never too far away.[2] While Burrows could easily handle himself in any fight, he was also cautious to follow procedure in order to ensure any wrongdoers felt the force of the law.

Things came to a head when Burrows encountered the Reverend Francis Lucius Carey late one night on Northgate Street. Carey was far from what could be considered to be a man of the cloth. He was a deeply connected man within the city and had a particular interest in those who inhabited the underworld of Chester. The Irish reverend was well known as a heavy drinker who had a reputation for carrying pistols and seemed determined to find whoever he was looking for at the Pied Bull coaching house.[3]

In his inebriated state, Carey was disturbing the peace late at night by banging on the Pied Bull's door and 'swearing that, while none should keep him out, any who refused to assist him in breaking in should be shot down forthwith'.[4] Burrows just so happened to be passing by as the commotion erupted. He could have just walked past Carey and gone home to be with Mary and Henry, but Burrows' sense of justice took firm hold of him. With the assistance of James Howell, one of Chester's watchmen, Burrows challenged the drunken Carey and removed him by force from the scene, placing him in a nearby watch-house.

The next morning, Carey was due to face the mayor of Chester and was bound to appear at the sessions. It was an appearance he would never attend. Instead, an incensed Carey would use his underworld connections to enact his revenge over Burrows in order to prevent him from giving any evidence to the sessions. William Wilson would be one of the men used in order to fulfil the reverend's fiendish plan.[5]

Wilson was a member of the much-feared press gang who served under Captain William Birchall, who was commanding the Chester region Sea Fencibles. Impressment, more colloquially known as 'the press', was a common feature in towns around the coastlines of Britain. It was a practice where the military could (and indeed, did) take men under forced conscription. This was a precarious time during the Napoleonic Wars and the navy in particular needed men urgently. Any man could be pressed between the ages of 18 to 55, but the tendency was to particularly press men with any seafaring experience. Chester, with its proximity to the River Dee, was a minor player in the importing and exporting of goods for the region and for that reason had plenty of men that could have been pressed.

However, Chester did not take kindly to Captain William Birchall and the members of his press gang. He had previously attempted to make his mark on the city in 1803 but would leave with his tail between his legs. His failure to form his own press gang within the boundaries of Chester meant that he brought his gang from nearby Liverpool. Men from Chester who would have wanted to avoid the press would volunteer their services to the local militia, otherwise known as the Royal Chester Artillery, in order to remain in the city. The Royal Chester was full of men who were desirable to Captain Birchall given their particular seafaring skills.

His gang signalled their intentions by pressing a well-known volunteer at the Royal Chester Artillery. Daniel Jackson may not have known it at the time but his forceful pressing would eventually lead to a riot as Cestrians fought for him to be released from their clutches. It was a mob that 'even the magistrates feared to face'. Such was the anger of the crowd that they 'broke open the city jail and rescued their comrade'.[6] Jackson was saved and the gang removed from the city, but that did not mean that everyone was still completely safe. Especially people who challenged individuals such as Reverend Carey.

Carey summoned members of Birchall's press gang to take Burrows. William Wilson would later admit to being one of the members of this group. According to a broadside released at the time of his execution, he made an unlikely confession regarding the city's executioner. It states that Wilson 'voluntarily mentioned his having been in the press gang at Chester at the time Burrows (now the public executioner) was taken by them; and said he was subsequently discharged by Captain Burchall [sic]'.[7]

Wilson's discharge was more than likely directly linked to his actions regarding Samuel Burrows. Following the events of 1803, the city had made their feelings about the press gang extremely clear. It would appear then that Carey went behind Birchall's back and summoned the gang directly from his own knowledge of its members.

It had just gone six o'clock in the morning. Burrows had already left his home to begin his long day of work. Mr Roberts of the Queen's Head on Bridge Street had ordered a freshly butchered pig from him and, eager to fulfil his duties, he headed to his workplace on the Shambles. With Henry still asleep, Mary used the opportunity of some peace to gather some essentials. It was just a normal Tuesday morning for the family but it would not take long for trouble to rear its ugly head. The press gang, including William Wilson, were heading straight to the Burrows' residence on Northgate Street. Mary followed but was soon seen by the gang and was 'accosted by O'Brien who said they have come for her husband and have them they would'. Mary, in a desperate attempt to save her husband, pleaded with the gang of nine men and stated that Samuel had gone out on business. That was not enough to deter the gang as they raided the Burrows' home searching for him. As she held her young son in her arms in order to protect him, the gang promptly left, leaving her home overturned.[8]

She urged Henry to be brave as she left him alone to go looking for Samuel. She knew he was at the Shambles even this early in the morning. Samuel was busy, he had just begun to butcher the carcass in front of him when the gang arrived searching for him. A scuffle began as Burrows tried to evade them but was swiftly overpowered. Mary, in a state of panic, ran towards the Shambles but 'before she arrived there learned that he had been taken by the Press Gang'. Desperately looking around the area, she caught sight of them and spotted them taking Samuel to the rendezvous before he could board the ship.[9]

Burrows himself later recalled that, 'Mr O'Brien and several members of the Gang ... Knocked him about and used him very cruelly.' With the beating complete, the gang then forcibly placed him in a 'black hole for a considerable time'. With Mary engaging the authorities of Chester, a search was quickly conducted and it would not take long to find Burrows. Battered by the press gang, he was found lying on the floor in a state of semi-consciousness. Mary described him as being 'knocked about badly' when she found him and immediately rushed to comfort her husband. With his blood varnishing the wood beneath him, and not knowing exactly where he was, he was helped up and removed.[10]

Mary was joined by Captain Birchall. He was a politically astute man who knew full well that the outcome would be ugly back in Chester, especially following what had happened only a year prior. Birchall demanded that Burrows be discharged from the rendezvous following a brief meeting with the ship's captain. Burrows was safe, albeit bruised and battered, and it was Mary who saved him. Mary was also quick to point the finger of blame at the Reverend Francis Lucius Carey, claiming that one of the members of the press gang told her that Burrows 'had been taken at the instigation of Francis Carey'.[11]

Carey kept his head down around Chester following the incident but his infamy meant that not many people had the courage to actually stand up against him. Rumours continued to circulate around town as to his responsibility for the illegal impressment of Burrows but for now Carey still harboured interests within the city. While his influence slowly ebbed away among members of the underworld, Carey aimed to garner influence alongside the exclusive gentleman of the city, who would not know him for who he truly was.

In his vain attempts to gain more gravitas within the city, he decided to join one of Chester's elite clubs. Known as 'The Honourable Incorporation of the King's Arms Kitchen', this exclusive gentlemen's club held influence within the city. It did, however, have one rule that they were prepared to break in order to have Carey as a member, that being that members of the clergy were not permitted to join. The minute book of the club states that: 'March 21st 1805: the Rev Lucius Carey was proposed by Mr Simpson and seconded by Sheriff Paul to become a member … and was unanimously accepted … the Town Clerk's fee being reserved. Afterwards expelled.'[12] His reason for his expulsion from the club has never been known but news of his misdemeanours regarding Burrows and others must have made its way to the ears of those who held influence. Carey is then never heard of again within the city records.

William Wilson had always been a naval man long before his involvement with Captain Birchall and the press gang. He had previously served under Admiral Sir George Rodney at the Battle of the Saintes during the American Revolutionary War in 1782 during his younger days and was keen to elaborate on his performance, declaring himself to be 'as bold a warrior as ever drawn a cutlass'.[13] The navy was all that Wilson knew and he was keen to continue in some way shape or form. Impressing recruits was something that he deemed necessary, especially with the intensification of the Napoleonic Wars that were still raging throughout the Continent.

Despite Wilson's continued work for the press gang, he would find himself in the unfortunate position of being pushed aside by

Captain Birchall. Perhaps it was because of his involvement in Chester and his forcible impressment of Burrows, but age was also against him. Approaching 70 years old, his services were no longer desirable. However, that did not seem to deter Wilson as he continued to impress men for naval service. Now he found himself claiming poor relief from his parish but his means were not for himself but to use the money in order to continue to ply men with drink in order to impress them into the service.

He approached Mr Butler, who was a respectable farmer and overseer of the poor within the parish of Tiverton. Wilson had applied for relief to the sum of £5 in order to use the money to impress potential sailors with ale. Needless to say, Mr Butler rejected his claim. It was a rejection that hit Wilson hard, especially as he was depending on that income in order to profit.[13]

On the evening of 15 October 1813, Mr Butler went to sleep without giving William Wilson much thought at all. Little did he know that Wilson had not stopped thinking about the unfairness of the situation that he had found himself in since his rejection of funds. He was not alone in feeling the same way. According to Wilson's confession for the crime he was about to commit, he did not act alone. Three women, all beggars, would also feel that a level of injustice was done to them and soon a plan came together in order to get revenge on the overseer of the poor.

The quartet went to Butler's farm as he slept. Two of the women set fire to his barn using tinder wrapped in a piece of rag. They then left Wilson by the hedge, where Joseph Ackerley came past him and spoke to him. As the fire slowly began to ignite, Wilson and his accomplices headed to Mr Fletcher's home, where they stayed for the rest of the night. With their evil work completed, they would have had no idea just how quickly the fire would spread.

The Butlers' servant-maid was alerted soon after the family went to bed at approximately eight o'clock that evening. Startled out of their slumber, they rushed out of the house to see their barn ablaze. They immediately set about extinguishing the fire and Butler's thoughts were taken over by

The Noose of Samuel Burrows

William Wilson and their exchange the previous day when he rejected his claim. In the heated confrontation, he remembered Wilson's threats and how he sarcastically wished that the barn would burn. It would be enough for the authorities to gather Wilson, although the women who he claimed had joined him were now nowhere to be found.[14]

Wilson was transferred to Chester Castle, where he would wait until his upcoming trial. During the trial itself, the judge constantly cautioned Wilson over his conduct. If Wilson believed that this would endear him to the jury as he constantly pleaded his innocence then he would be sorely mistaken. He was found guilty and the judge opted to sentence him to death.

Burrows slept soundly on the evening before the upcoming execution of William Wilson. He returned home feeling slightly merry following a session at the Boot Inn on Eastgate Row only a short walk from his home. He giggled to himself as he crept into the bedroom to see Mary sound asleep. Rather than wake her, he tiptoed his way across the floor, slid into bed, and quickly drifted off to sleep. Wilson did not have the luxury of intoxication to aid his slumber but nevertheless drifted into a deep sleep himself. Over the previous days since his fateful sentencing, he had accepted his upcoming date with destiny with a level of indifference. At the age of 70, Wilson knew that he would meet his maker sooner rather than later anyway. All that consumed him was whether or not Burrows would recognise him.

Matthew Hudson, the constable of Chester Castle, had tried to petition for Wilson's stay of execution but all he could receive was a brief respite. Hudson, in writing his response to the failed petition, said:

> The poor unfortunate man seems grateful at having a little more time allotted him to prepare himself, that he does not expect a conditional pardon, but could it be done he would

ever pray, in consideration of having a daughter upwards of 20 years old living with some respectable relations in this county.[15]

Despite this last desperate plea for pardon on behalf of Wilson, Hudson heard nothing back on this occasion. While it gave Wilson a couple of weeks longer to live, it also gave Burrows and the rest of Chester more time to prepare in the knowledge that the petition had failed.

W.C. Jones owned a printing business on King Street in Chester. His staff had been up for most of the night preparing the broadside for Wilson's execution. Hundreds were produced and were now drying on the makeshift lines that scattered the premises. When the staff arrived first thing in the morning, they just needed to be taken down and distributed among those who would sell them. By now, the sellers knew the routes of the procession that would lead the condemned through the streets of Chester, and with his execution scheduled for midday, it gave them plenty of time to mingle within the crowds of Bridge Street and Watergate Street armed with their tales of criminality. As they made their final checks and began to pack their bags, Wilson was already awake.

Wilson enjoyed a hearty breakfast on the morning of 28 May 1814. Indeed, for a man claiming poor relief, it would have probably felt more like a feast. He had asked if he could take some more with him as he was paraded through the streets on his journey to New City Gaol. It was an unlikely request but given the circumstances, Matthew Hudson obliged by offering him some extra bread and cheese.[16] Throughout the morning he continued to claim his innocence, suggesting that the authorities sought after the women who were there with him that night. The gaolers were eager for him to become the city's problem as they escorted him out of the gaol, where they would meet the city of Chester's officials at the Gloverstone.

Samuel Burrows also enjoyed a breakfast lovingly prepared by Mary. He was still fast asleep as his wife's day began. She could hear his snores as she was busy preparing the fire that she lit to take any chill away from her home. Leaving to fetch water, she could still hear her husband as she closed the door behind her. It would not take her long to return as she prepared breakfast and poured some water into a bowl for his morning wash. When Burrows awoke, everything was ready for him, from food to the clothes that he wore that day. It was a routine that she had become used to, especially on execution days. With Samuel now awake all he had to do was get himself ready before the short walk down Watergate Street in order to make his own preparations for Wilson's day of reckoning.

Wilson laughed as he was exchanged at the Gloverstone. Those convicted by the country but then later executed in the city had been exchanged there since the time Henry VII sat on the throne. In 1506 Henry granted Chester its 'Great Charter', which constituted the city to be a county in its own right. From the County Gaol at the Castle, Wilson would make his way through the streets of Chester to his eventual destination of New City Gaol. Wilson had a strong military escort waiting for him at the Gloverstone. He was reported to have remarked that the situation was laughable, suggesting that they 'were making as much fuss as if they were a hundred men to be hanged'.[17]

On board the cart, he slowly made his way through the cobbled streets of Chester. As people clambered to catch a glimpse of him all they could see was an elderly man snacking on bread and cheese as his cart passed them by.[18] Sellers of broadsides from across Chester were busy hawking the streets in an attempt to find buyers interested in the man who went past them. Despite the preparations, there was never as much interest in someone like Wilson when compared to murderers. With some copies left unsold, the sellers returned to the printers, who hastily encouraged them to head back to the streets as some copies could still be sold at the event itself.

As the crowd followed Wilson to the gaol, Burrows was already there putting the finishing touches on the noose that would hang him. It had almost become second nature to Burrows but at this particular moment of time he had no idea that it would be the only noose that he would make all year. With Wilson receiving his final sacrament, Burrows looked at the gathering crowd. He noticed that there were not as many as those who witnessed the execution of Edith Morrey but either way he could still put on a show for the ones who had shown up. All he could do now was to wait until he was called to tie the condemned man's hands and then escort him towards his gallows.

Samuel Burrows was more than prepared for Wilson by the time the call finally came. Pinioning a criminal could go either way. Some accepted their fate and in that case it was easy to do. The ones that caused a fuss or began to panic would require more physical restraint. It wouldn't matter either way to Burrows but before him Wilson was the epitome of calm, offering his hands to the hangman. Burrows looked at Wilson all but briefly before going to work to restrain him. Wilson nervously swallowed in the faint hope that Burrows did not recognise him.

Their exchange would be brief on the gallows above the New City Gaol but for Burrows it was simply just another job. When Burrows finally saw Wilson he vaguely recognised him but could not pinpoint exactly where their paths had crossed before. Wilson certainly knew Burrows though and upon seeing him decided to remain silent. Now was not the time to rock the boat; all Wilson could do was hope that the drop would not be too painful.

Burrows placed the hood over Wilson's head and as he was plunged into darkness it heightened his other senses. He could hear the baying crowd beneath him with more intensity than before. He could also hear Burrows heavily breathing into his ear as he reached for his noose. As he applied it over his head Wilson felt the sharp thrust as the hangman pulled down on it to tighten it around his neck. As he inhaled with fear, Wilson felt the pulse from his jugular vein pulsating stronger as he began to realise the severity of his situation. To make doubly sure, Burrows pulled on his noose again. Wilson could hear Burrows muttering as his sweat trickled from his brow inside the hood. Whatever Burrows said, Wilson could not comprehend the words fully. He felt the rough hand of Burrows on his frail skin as Burrows placed a handkerchief between Wilson's fingers. Wilson felt another tug on the noose as Burrows leaned in menacingly and told him to drop it when he was ready to depart the Earth.

The hangman then walked towards his lever and waited for his signal. He was still trying to recall how he knew Wilson but at the same moment he knew that for whatever reason he was about to launch him into eternity either way. In his mind, Wilson was just another condemned criminal to add to his ever-growing collection. It would only be when Burrows eventually heard about Wilson's involvement with the press gang later on the streets of Chester that he would finally remember him. For now, though, he watched the handkerchief intensely with a focused eagerness to release the drop.

Wilson would be one of Burrows' more fortunate victims. As he let go of the handkerchief and Burrows released the mechanism, he would drop almost instantly to his death. Perhaps it was his age that spared him from a longer asphyxiation than usually witnessed by the Cestrian crowd. His elderly infirm body simply did not have the strength to fight for his life in the way that a younger person could. Either way, he was now dead and left to hang for an hour as the handkerchief Burrows gave him fluttered through the Chester sky.

Chapter 9

The Devil's Bank Notes

The Execution of Joseph Allen
New City Gaol, Chester, 1817

AS JOSEPH ALLEN sat in the condemned cell at New City Gaol the gravity of the situation he found himself in was beginning to feel more and more real. His meeting with Samuel Burrows would be brief and for those waiting to see him on the gallows, he knew it would be a mixture of sorrow and excitement. He knew there would be many in the crowd who would at least see him as a victim but there would also be those who saw him as a man who took an honest mistake too far by enriching himself with what would later be named in a pamphlet distributed across London in 1820 as 'Satan's Bank Note'.[1]

Receiving his last rites, his thoughts would have swirled around his head about how something so simple could get out of hand so quickly. Allen would have been hoping for some last-minute reprieve but as he approached the steps towards Burrows, he knew that that time had passed. For Allen, like many who climbed those fateful steps across the country, his crime was one of a mixture of greed, ignorance, or in some cases, abject poverty, where a gift from the devil came in many forms. Now it was time for his soul to depart as Satan waited patiently in the wings for his reward.

Allen would become another successful conviction for the Bank of England in their battle against the counterfeiters and utterers of newly distributed £1 and £2 notes that were rushed into circulation during the Napoleonic Wars. The war with France was taking its toll on all aspects of the country regardless of social standings. It was a policy that would have grave consequences for thousands of individuals and was heightened further by William Pitt the Younger's latest policy of the introduction of Income Tax in 1799. Yet it was the introduction of lower-value pound notes that would be the undoing of Joseph Allen.

Gold withdrawals were becoming a major issue in 1797 as fears of a French invasion swept across the country. In order to deal with this, the British government banned the withdrawal of gold as currency and urged the Bank of England to find another means where currency could be distributed while keeping the gold reserves within the bank itself. The Bank of England had to tread carefully as smaller denominations were needed. With this in mind, the bank rushed forward with plans to introduce smaller amounts of the British pound in the form of bank notes. Prior to this, the Bank of England had produced notes from the value of £5 upwards but the need to stabilise the economy meant that they hastily rushed the production of £1 and £2 notes. The haste to do so meant that these cruder notes were far easier to counterfeit and the smaller amounts than previously produced meant that they were far easier to circulate.[2]

Soon, gangs of forgers would begin their work creating counterfeit £1 and £2 notes. While this was considered to be a capital crime, the idea of counterfeiting notes was nothing new. The only difference between the eighteenth and the early nineteenth century was the sheer scale of the offence. The crime of 'uttering', or the distribution of fake money, was a capital crime dating back to 1725. But while the Bank of England may have unwittingly allowed for the explosion of the crime with their new notes from 1797, it was also their responsibility to track down any forged notes and those who either made or distributed them. It was a responsibility that the bank took extremely seriously, using any means at their disposal, and with both crimes considered to be capital crimes, they had a whole series of punishments at their disposal.

Thomas Glover was perhaps one of the busiest men in England during this time. As the Bank of England's note inspector, he would travel the country inspecting forged notes at almost every instance.[3] His expert knowledge of banknotes could determine one's guilt. He was only one of the invaluable resources that the bank would use in order to catch the culprits. The other, and possibly more formidable, resource used was the law itself.

Where possible, deals with those who were caught uttering notes were made. The process was relatively simple. The bank would ask those who were caught to tell them where they got the notes from and from there hopefully they could get to the main source. Deals would include a lighter sentence including transportation or time in prison rather than the ultimate punishment of death.

One such deal by the Bank of England was attempted in Chester long before Joseph Allen faced his own trial. It would serve as a warning to all within the area that it would be better for them to cooperate.

Mary Lloyd found herself in a terrible situation. She was a widow with a young family to look after. In Georgian Britain this was about as bad as it could possibly get. Relying heavily on poor relief, it would still be almost impossible for her to make ends meet. That was until her encounter with a forger who encouraged her to utter counterfeit notes. When she was eventually caught and put on trial in October 1800 there would be only one outcome. For Mary's actions, she was now facing death by hanging at Chester's Gallows Hill in Boughton.

As Mary awaited her impending execution, there was plenty of action going on behind the scenes as the Bank of England's solicitors pushed for her punishment. The Sheriff of Chester Castle, where Mary was incarcerated, felt some sympathy towards her situation. Believing her to be worthy of some mercy, he wrote to the Duke of Portland explaining her case. Another letter was also written. James Mansfield, the Chief Justice for Chester, explained his decision to execute Lloyd, saying that 'he knew nothing about the case that merited a respite'. However, Mansfield asked that the bank should write to the Sheriff if they thought that there was any reason to reconsider the decision.[4]

The bank duly replied to the Sheriff and it would turn out that deals had previously been made with Lloyd. She had repeatedly been given the opportunity by the bank to appear as a crown witness against the forgers. However, Mary had declined this offer 'in the most insolent manner'.[5] In doing so, the bank declared Lloyd to be a willing accomplice in the crime and that it was only when she received her death sentence that she had finally wanted to reveal her sources.

The next correspondence on 22 October 1800 was sent by the Sheriff to the bank's solicitors, which revealed that Lloyd had been executed. She was now the cautionary tale to those in the Chester area that uttering illicit bank notes came at the ultimate price.

Two years later, Thomas Rushton was facing a similar fate. A former brewer from Liverpool, he too had been uttering counterfeit notes. However, in his case, he was more than prepared to talk. Convicted in Chester and sentenced to fourteen years' transportation, he wrote to the bank's solicitors at Freshfields:

> I before mention'd in a Letter to Mr. Ward, Constable of the Castle Chester, that the one Pound Notes was hid in Liverpool, I mentioned the Place where they were hid and who I supposed found them. The particulars of that information in my Letter has I suppose been laid before you or the directors of the Bank of England – if these notes can be found, I can point out I conceive how the Person I had them from may be convicted, who is one of the Makers and now in London, I have got the original note they were made from.[6]

The fate of Rushton was far different to that of Lloyd. While his transportation to Van Diemen's Land would still go ahead, he at least had the opportunity to make a new life for himself. Rushton would be swiftly pardoned in 1804 and would never serve his fourteen years. Instead, Rushton and his brewing knowledge would be used to its fullest as he was swiftly relocated to Australia, going on to become a key member of the colony's new expanding brewing community as the government used beer in its fight against illegal shipments of spirits, especially rum.[7]

These two opposing stories allow us to know just how hard the Bank of England fought against the scourge of counterfeiting in the county of Cheshire but it also shows us that negotiating with the bank did have its advantages. Those who remained silent such as Mary Lloyd would face the fullest force of the law.

The case of Mary Lloyd would have reverberated around the county, and indeed the country as a whole, yet the issue facing the Bank of England was still growing. Joseph Allen would simply become its latest case and he would be prosecuted in the same way as hundreds of other accused criminals across the kingdom. In 1817, the same year as Allen was facing his trial, a total of 142 other such cases were being brought forward for the crime of uttering and counterfeiting banknotes, involving a total of £29,521 in counterfeit notes. Of the 142 individuals prosecuted that year, 32 just like Allen would face the noose with a further 95 being convicted of possession facing either hefty stints in prison or the more favoured option of transportation.[8]

If the cases of Lloyd and Rushton were a warning to anyone uttering illegal bank notes then it was a warning that Joseph Allen did not heed. The 39-year-old farmer from Crowton was facing a jury of his peers at Chester Assizes and he knew that some kind of punishment was awaiting him.

Suspicions first came to light regarding Allen when forged notes were passed to Mr Nicolson, a solicitor from Warrington. Samuel Woodward was paid £9 by Allen for joinery work completed at his new farm. Every note that he received from Allen was a £1 denomination. Woodward, not thinking that anything was particularly wrong with the transaction, then used £8 over a period of time to pay a Mrs Okell for potatoes. Woodward and Okell were unwitting participants in Allen's uttering and it was only when Mrs Okell attempted to use the notes herself that she realised what had happened.[9]

All of her notes were returned to her by traders refusing to accept them. Confused, Mrs Okell sought help and approached Mr Nicolson. It was only then that he revealed to her that the notes that she had in her hand were potential forgeries. Now, Mr Nicolson went on his own hunt to find the source of the illicit notes. It would not take long to track them down to one main source in the area.

Joseph Allen was described in court as 'a character of extraordinary goodness' who was married with seven young children. Prior to his trial, he was the kind of man the whole village admired greatly and widely trusted. As a businessman, his 'character stood so exceedingly high, that large sums of money had been advanced to him without any other security being required from him but his word'.[10]

As Allen stood before the jury he must have believed that his good character would hold some sway. After all, it was not as if he had forged the notes himself. Instead, he acquired them elsewhere. How could it even be proved that he had done this intentionally? However, any hope that he had that things would go his way soon came crashing down as Thomas Glover, the inspector of notes for the Bank of England, gave his evidence. What was revealed took any gleam of Allen's good character away.

Glover revealed exactly how the forged notes were different from legitimate notes in circulation. He quickly identified that the ink used for the forgeries had more brown than black ink in an attempt to make it look more frequently used and that the paper used to produce the note was harsher than the real ones used by the bank. Of all the notes that were gathered during the investigation, more than 100 were proven to have been uttered by Allen. While Allen used the notes freely, it also appeared that he was enriching himself with them rather than being the victim of obtaining these notes through an illicit source.

Allen's farm provided further proof that he was profiting from the uttered notes. This was not a simple case of survival through tough times such as Mary Lloyd, but of a man who knew exactly what he was doing. In the previous year, Allen had rented a farm where he lived and worked that was valued at £30 per annum. Yet as his uttering grew, he later moved to another property, which was valued at between £200 to £300 per annum. It was a move that all but sealed his eventual fate when the authorities came to visit him.

The Devil's Bank Notes

Once inside his property, constables found fourteen £1 notes on his desk. The backs were marked with the name 'Joseph Jelly'. More notes were found in a drawer that were torn yet perfectly clean and new. They had no appearance of ever being in circulation. It was enough to apprehend him.[11]

What Allen did not know was that the name on the back of his notes would also be damning evidence against him at his trial. Joseph Jelly and Samuel Allen were responsible for printing the notes. Allen was Joseph's brother and it was this family connection that made it all too easy for the notes to be produced and uttered into the local economy. As the two men saw their fortunes change, more and more notes were produced, with Joseph Allen's reputation within his community being used to gain the trust of those who he dealt with at farmers' markets across Manchester and Cheshire.

Joseph Jelly and Samuel Allen had already been arrested and placed on trial by the time Joseph Allen was arrested himself. Jelly was tried in Lancaster but subsequently escaped from his cell. Samuel was transported to Van Diemen's Land for fourteen years for his offence. With this in mind, Joseph must have been expecting a similar punishment as his five-hour trial was drawing to its conclusion.[12]

Sir William Garrow, the Chief Justice of Chester, waited for the jury to reach their decision. Finding Allen guilty, the court erupted, forcing the Cryer of the Court to silence them. Placing a black cap on his head, Garrow stared at Allen, who began to sob and grow ever more agitated. Sir William Garrow, in a sombre tone, revealed his sentence saying:

> To see a man that had filled such a respectable situation and guilty of such a great crime, it is now up to God to show mercy as there is no chance of any on earth.[13]

Sentenced to death, Allen returned to Chester Castle to await his date with Samuel Burrows.

The Noose of Samuel Burrows

Burrows was experiencing a lull when it came to his regular executions. Since his meeting with William Wilson, he had hardly appeared on top of Chester City Gaol for nearly two years. Times were becoming difficult for the Burrows family, with money desperately running low. Yet he was not alone by any stretch of the imagination. The previous year was known as 'the year without summer' as 1816 experienced the wettest and most unpredictable weather seen. The impact on Chester was also felt as yet another poor harvest forced inflation to spike. A desperate situation for many prior to 1816 had now grown even worse. Like many, the Burrows family were also impacted. As the price of food rose ever higher, his retainer was becoming increasingly worthless and far from what he was accustomed to.[14]

Samuel had kept a close eye on the Joseph Allen case. He would find himself hanging around the Golden Eagle pub, just a stone's throw away from the Castle, listening to the conversations of those who had attended the trial. Returning home, he would let Mary know everything that was happening even though he knew that there was a greater likelihood of an alternative punishment to execution. Both knew exactly how important it was for Sammy to return to the gallows. With money rapidly running out, it had become a case of survival for the Burrows.

When the announcement came that Allen was to be executed, Burrows breathed a faint sigh of relief yet he knew that there would be many who would probably try to prevent it. The situation was becoming more frequent. He opted to give it a few days before properly thinking about his return to the top of Chester City Gaol. When the death warrant for Allen was finally released, Burrows got busy again. He tested the drop a few times once the gallows were erected in order to ensure that it was still working properly after all these years. With the lever in his hand, he felt good about himself. It was a mixture of excitement and relief but finally Burrows was back and the whole city could see him in action once again.

On Saturday, 10 May 1817, Joseph Allen awoke for the final time before being given a hearty breakfast. Receiving religious comfort, he was reported to have said, 'Dear, dear, what a great change I shall shortly undergo.'[15] He would reside in the Castle until midday in order to be exchanged at the Gloverstone before his slow parade through the streets.

Travelling down Bridge Street, Allen could see the crowds but, unlike other execution parades, this one felt more sedated. Instead of cheers, he saw faces full of sorrow. It was almost as if those who lined the streets felt more sorry for him than other criminals who had passed them by. Even the ballad mongers who roamed the streets sang in lowered tones when reciting their sorrowful ballad of Joseph Allen. Everyone was feeling the economic stresses for themselves following 1816. The empathy was genuine from the Cestrian onlookers and, given the opportunity, many would have done the same as Allen. To many, he was simply doing whatever he could to survive.

Burrows, of course, did not see things the same way. This was his livelihood and whatever people thought about the law was irrelevant to him. Allen had broken the law and it really was as simple as that. As the crowd arrived to witness Allen's final moments, they had no time for Burrows' usual antics. Regardless of what he believed, he was savvy enough to sense the mood of the crowd was firmly against him.

When Burrows pulled the lever and Allen dropped, there was almost silence, which was eventually broken with small sounds of weeping. It did not take the crowd too long to disperse as Allen was left to hang for another hour before eventually being cut down. Burrows was told to be careful with the body and to place it in the coffin that had been bought by some gentlemen from Weaverham. With help, Burrows placed the coffin on a hearse, where it was taken back to be with his family before burial.[16]

For Burrows, it was an odd feeling. It was a nice coffin, unlike some of the others he had previously seen, and to see the coffin slowly move away from him in a specially made hearse had taken him aback. Perhaps the crowd was right, perhaps not all crimes are equal. Burrows did not dwell on it too long. It was time for some much-needed cash and a well-deserved drink or two.

Joseph Allen's family was left all but destitute from the moment of his arrest. The larger farm that he had rented from the uttered money was too large for the young family to manage and with no means of paying the larger rent, they were forced to move out. The community gathered to help them form a collection to make sure that they were in a better financial situation. When Joseph arrived back in Weaverham the community ensured that he was buried in the churchyard. There was no ill will towards the family or to Allen himself for his crime especially when, only one week after she had buried her son, Joseph's mother passed away with what the local community said was a broken heart.[17]

Chapter 10

The Road to Near Ruin

The Execution of John Connor
Galltegfa, Ruthin, 1822

BURROWS HAD FIRMLY established himself as the city's executioner. With his new-found infamy and more money in his pocket than he had ever had in his life, he had also found a new way to spend it. Samuel was always a drinker but now he had taken it to even more extreme levels as he was becoming more dependent on it.

Perhaps it was the nature of his work. Maybe it was part of the comedown following another performance, or possibly, it was always there, his demon lurking in the background waiting for his moment of weakness to explode. Either way, more and more stories were emerging about him, and his conduct as the city's 'finisher of the law' was being questioned more and more by the authorities that hired him in the first place.

His antics on the gallows were becoming less popular, with the local newspapers showing their disdain towards the city's hangman. The execution of William Rickington and Ralph Ellis in 1820 highlighted that Burrows was becoming a polarising figure. There was a level of sympathy for Ellis, who was found guilty of burglary in Ellesmere Port. As the 19-year-old was being spiritually prepared, Burrows was entertaining the masses with his usual form of dark comedy, which bordered on the horrific. The local newspaper reported that:

> In affixing the ropes, the fellow who fills the disgusting office tied the length of them, by applying with the utmost Sang

Froid the noose of one to his own neck; some person in the crowd cried out 'For Shame, Shame!' The fellow repeated the motion, smiling at his own callosity of feeling.[1]

His fondness for alcohol had taken over. Often conducting executions while inebriated, Burrows was becoming an embarrassment to the local authorities yet he saw no issue with his own behaviour. In his mind, it was what the multitude wanted to see and a few naysayers were not going to spoil the show for everyone else. What Burrows did not take into account was that while he was tolerated, he was far from admired for his lack of professionalism, which was slowly getting worse depending on how much he had drunk prior to ascending the gallows.

In some cases, rumours began to circle that Burrows was being forced to spend a night in the cells of New City Gaol prior to executing the condemned so that he would be sober enough to carry out his duties. The rumours began to spread all over the county as to the state of their executioner. Even those about to face Burrows were beginning to find it amusing. On 13 September 1823, Edward Clarke made a joke about the state of Burrows as he was facing his own trip to the gallows.

Found guilty of highway robbery, the condemned Clarke turned to his gaolers and his words were echoed around the country as the press were quick to publish what he had said. The rumour that he had heard was that the powers that be had finally fired Burrows due to his constant distasteful exhibitions on the gallows while drunk. Clarke was reported as saying: 'I've heard they've turned Sam off – I know him very well; where is he now? I suppose I shall have a fresh one?'[2]

Unknown to Clarke, Burrows was still around. Instead of firing Burrows, the authorities allowed him to continue on the condition that he was relatively sober enough to carry out his duties. While what Clarke had heard had a grain of truth, it was far from the whole story as others told their embellished version. Burrows was in a cell, sleeping off the alcohol he had previously consumed, and was now busy preparing his gallows for Clarke's execution. Of course, Burrows would still perform his regular shenanigans on the platform but it was with a little bit more restraint.

The drinking that Burrows was now conducting was regular and excessive. His need for attention, given his position as the city's executioner, had consumed him. In his mind, he was a celebrity wherever he went. However, his need for drink and attention almost cost him his own life when he was asked to take a trip to Ruthin in order to execute an Irishman by the name of John Connor.

The execution of Connor came at a good time for Burrows. The previous year, 1821, was one of the worst professional years he could remember. His noose was only used once and that was for the execution of Samuel Healey, who was convicted of highway robbery. The job naturally came with its ebbs and flows but on the whole Burrows had been constantly busy. It had been a struggle in 1816 as Burrows' noose gathered dust for the whole year. While his retainer paid him well enough, it was the actual executions themselves that brought in the real money. However, Burrows often forgot to save his money in preparation for any lean years. Instead, he would drink it away in the belief that another execution would only be weeks away once the Assize had assembled. However, things were beginning to change within the kingdom. Transportation was becoming a much more popular method of justice rather than execution. He was also becoming all too well aware that there were some slipping through his noose. Many were having their sentences appealed and those who had previously been condemned to hang by his noose were now enjoying a stay of execution in favour of transportation. For Burrows, it was an added frustration to what was once a very lucrative affair.

Wales was always in full view of Burrows whenever he was on top of his scaffold at the New City Gaol. Facing west, from his vantage point he could see more than most; the meandering River Dee, the shipyards, and newly built canals that had seen the city survive, although only just, as cities like Liverpool enjoyed the industrial boom of the early nineteenth century. While Chester might have been left behind in comparison to the emerging metropolises, it still had plenty to offer and was growing as a tourist destination filled with retail and commerce. The hustle and bustle of all that was a million miles away from where Burrows stood. Behind him were the cheese markets of the Linenhall and a vibrant but quant city but in front of him, the mystery of Wales with the peak of Moel Famau sculpting the spectacular landscape in front of him. It was no wonder that the city was beginning to attract so many tourists with views like that to explore. Yet, Wales was somewhere that Burrows had never bothered to venture himself; that was until he was summoned to the Exchange in Northgate Street.

The Exchange was Chester's administrative centre.[3] It was also where Burrows would be summoned in order to receive his instructions for any impending executions. His orders could come from anywhere and anyone who required his services. If he was needed at either of Chester's gaols in order to deliver corporal punishment to prisoners then it was part of his job that also needed to be conducted. However, the city could also offer his services to other jurisdictions that needed a man like Burrows. The City of Chester would receive some much-needed additional income by loaning out their hangman as and when required. For Burrows, it meant that he would be a bit busier venturing around the country rather than solely being dependent on his work in Chester. It was welcome news for him, especially with more and more death warrants being converted into travelling tickets as the 'Bloody Code' was slowly being challenged.

Denbighshire had asked the city for their assistance with regard to an upcoming execution of their own in Ruthin. For Burrows, it would be the first of many occasions that his services would lead him away from Chester. To him, the trip to Ruthin would have felt like an exciting excursion, but given the rather sparse previous year of 1821, when his noose went practically unused, it was also a welcome payday.

The trip included expenses, which was a welcome relief to the hangman. Stopping at coach houses in order to replenish the horses with rest, food and water also gave him the chance to replenish himself and without using his own money. The journey was long with constant changes in elevation that Burrows would not have been used to given the relative

Above left: A likeness of Samuel Burrows. (*The Chester Courant*, 1826)

Above right: The newly erected gaol next to the infirmary in 1810. (Steve Howe)

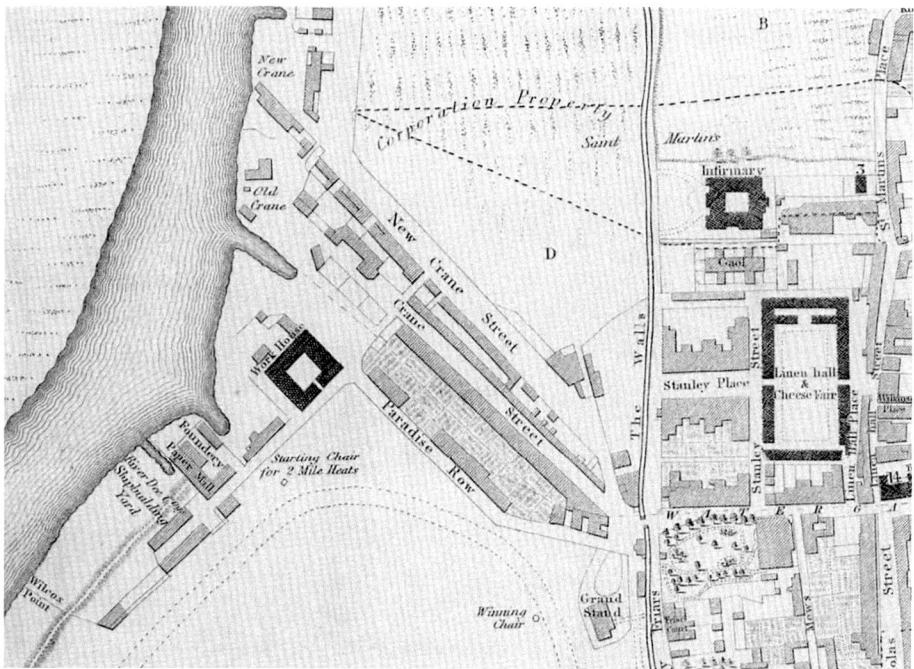

The area around the New City Gaol includes the Infirmary, Linen Hall, Racecourse, and Workhouse. Map of Chester, 1833 by John Wood. (The National Library of Wales)

The Rows, Chester, by Thomas Webster, 1807. (Yale Center For British Art)

White Friars, Chester, 1831, by George Sidney Shepherd. (The Art Institute of Chicago)

Part of Chester Castle, Byrne's 'Britannia Depicta', 1810. (Yale Center For British Art)

Bridge Street, Chester, 1821, from Lithographic Impressions of Sketches From Nature, Charles Joseph Hullmandel. (The Art Institute of Chicago)

Bridge of Sighs, Chester. (Author)

Northgate Street, Exchange, Fish and Vegetable Market, Chester. (ChesterWiki)

Above: Depiction of Shambles in Northgate Street, Chester.

Right: Reward poster for arson at William Radcliffe's warehouse.

Below: Shrewsbury Gaol gatehouse. (Author)

Above left: Beaumaris Gaol. (Author)

Above right: A lithograph of Judge John Gurney. (WikiCommons)

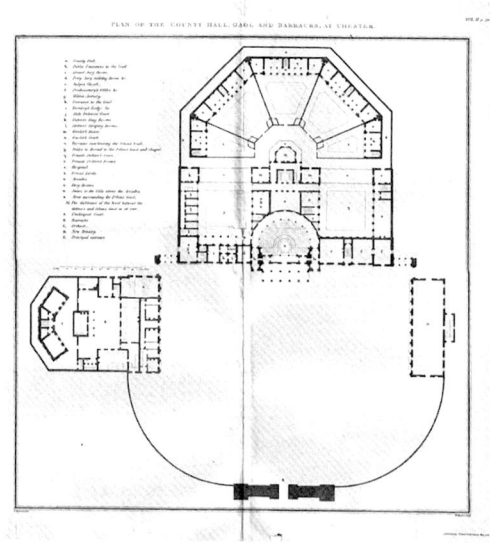

Above left: A lithograph of Griffith Rowlands, surgeon at Chester Infirmary responsible for anatomy before Dr Owen Titley. (Llyfrgell Genedlaethol Cymru – The National Library of Wales)

Above right: Plan of County Hall, Gaol and Barracks, Chester Castle by J. Harrison, engraved by W. Warner and published by Cadell & Davies, 1 May 1809. (ChesterWiki)

Broadside: 'John Lomas: The Barbarous Murderer of Mr. Morrey; of Hankelow, near Nantwich, Cheshire, was executed opposite the City Gaol, in Chester, on Monday, August 24, 1812'. (Harvard Law School Library, Harvard University)

The short walk to the gallows undertaken by William Griffith and Samuel Burrows, Beaumaris Gaol. (Author)

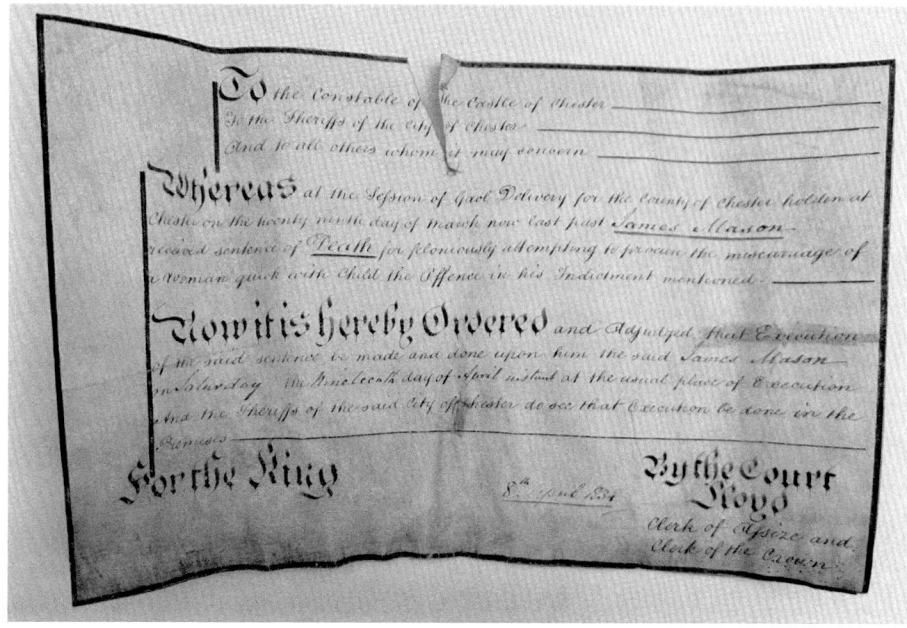

The death warrant for James Mason, 1834. (Chester Records Office)

Chester Cathedral, South East Graveyard by Thomas Annan, 1900. (Yale University)

The Road to Near Ruin

flatness of Cheshire in comparison. As he gazed around the open fields and mountainous areas he felt overwhelmed by their beauty, the quietness and most importantly, the sheer magnitude of the rolling hills and mysterious mountains as fog slowly crawled around them. Down the elevation of the valley lay Ruthin. With his journey nearly complete and his lungs filled with fresh air, he was not quite ready to rest. He felt a vigour like he had not experienced before.

The Red Lion Inn was a perfect place for the authorities of Denbighshire to house him, or so they thought.[4] Just over the road, Ruthin Gaol was only a few steps away should the condemned man need any brutish treatment beforehand. Unfortunately, they had no idea about the man that they hired and his fondness for drink. With expenses still left to spend, Burrows quickly headed to his room, threw his belongings to the ground, and then hastily went back downstairs to get himself the first of many drinks.

It would not take long for trouble to occur, especially with a now inebriated Burrows in full swing. Burrows had not taken the dire situation into account as he began to gloat about his profession to strangers. Bragging to others, Burrows had no idea that the condemned man waiting for his execution had friends looking to put an end to the executioner himself. They just needed to wait for their opportunity. Burrows had no idea of the danger that he actually found himself in, as John Connor's allies kept an eye on their prey.

John Connor came to Wales from Wexford in Ireland. While not much has been said about how long he was actually in Wales, we can assume that he had been there long enough to form a plan that would ensure a lucrative robbery. Standing 6ft 2in tall, Connor's imposing figure would have made anyone who approached him do so with an element of trepidation. A ballad written soon after his execution tells us more about his crime.

Ballad writers would gather as much information as they possibly could in order to compose their ditties. Sourcing the latest newspapers, broadsides, or even just local hearsay, the ballad writer would then form their poetic lyrics into songs that would be distributed to any prepared to pay for it. Ballads were popular and the greater the crime, the greater the warning of execution that was needed in order to remind individuals about the repercussions for such crimes.

The Ballad of John Connor was sung and written in Welsh. Composed by John Jones in nearby Holywell and using his native tongue, he presented a version of the crime that acted as a warning to any who were seeking to emulate Connor's deeds. Yet, with as much information as he could muster, Jones and his version of the crime is a fairly accurate one.

The ballad claims that Connor did not act alone in the audacious highway robbery that he would subsequently be executed for. Witnesses at his trial claim that they saw Connor with another man who was unidentified during the case. J. Jones claims that he was aided by William Thomas, yet when asked at trial who his accomplice was, Connor said nothing.

The two men had been keeping a watch in the village of Hanmer approximately 12 miles south-east of Wrexham. Overseers of the poor relief in the village made regular journeys to Wrexham in order to send money to the town. Connor and Thomas, according to this ballad, were keeping a watchful eye on them and spotted their patterns. Their aim was clear, to kill the officers responsible for taking the relief to Wrexham and steal the money.

There was, of course, a valid reason as to why Connor and Thomas sought to kill the officers. Both highway robbery and murder were punishable by death. Fully knowing this, the two men knew that if they were caught then a trip to the gallows was coming regardless of whether or not the officers survived. Killing them, they thought, would at least remove the possibility of witnesses who could later identify them at any potential trial.

Jones claimed that before the robbery Connor and Thomas waited for their prey at a local inn and while they waited had a stiff drink in order to summon the courage for what they were about to do. The inn was where they would find the two officers who frequently stopped there for their own refreshments. Little did the officers know that they were being watched.

The Road to Near Ruin

Jones' ballad did not leave much to the imagination with its descriptive prose as the two men went after the officers as they left the inn. Jones stated that:

> The two villainous evil murderers,
> They went after them without losing time.
> After catching them, they told them
> That they wanted their property.[5]

Attacking the officers, both Connor and Thomas believed that they had left them for dead and took the money with them before heading to Wrexham themselves. While they believed that they had got away with their crime, little did they know that the officers were still alive and crawled into a nearby field to escape any further reprisals. Connor was later caught, with Jones stating that his clothes still had the officers' blood on them which was later used as evidence against him.

According to one report, the prosecution alleged that perhaps four individuals were involved in the robbery that would see Connor hang. William Thomas was alleged to have been seen on numerous occasions following the robbery and arrest of his friend. Thomas's wife was also later arrested and imprisoned for uttering base coin yet revealed nothing of her husband's whereabouts.

William Thomas, on the other hand, was never caught at the time the ballad was sung around northern Wales. He found himself on the run but possibly knew about the fate of John Connor. He was due to be executed for the highway robbery and it was only because the two officers were still alive to testify against him.

Burrows was now drunk and eager to be the centre of attention at the Red Lion in Ruthin. Patrons of the inn were also curious to see exactly how Burrows would execute someone and had urged him to demonstrate how he would do it. Never one to shy away from a challenge, Burrows did exactly that and rushed back to his room to gather a noose. Returning to cheers, Burrows was in his element. The locals liked him and he was in the mood to entertain them.

Finding a beam along the inn's ceiling, Burrows slung his noose over it and then tied the remaining rope to a strong table. Rather than seeking a volunteer, Burrows proceeded to use the noose on himself as he stood on a stool. He put his own neck into the noose and tightened it firmly. More cheers came as the locals looked on and raised their glasses. Burrows was now in an awkward position and completely defenceless. It was the perfect opportunity to kill the hangman.

Henry Caddock saw his moment and casually walked over to Burrows, who was now wobbling on his stool in order to maintain his balance. Caddock then kicked the stool from under Burrows, who dropped a few inches and it was enough for the noose to start strangling him. A panicking Burrows then grabbed the noose with his hands in a vain attempt to relieve his neck from the force of the rope but even he would have known that unless someone actually came to his aid then he would be struggling for a while to free himself.[6]

The locals quickly turned on Caddock, forcing him to the ground as Thomas Humphreys reached for his knife and cut Burrows down. Coughing and trying to get his breath back, Burrows now finally knew how it felt for himself. He was OK but severely shaken. More drink was needed to steady his nerves. Caddock was thrown out of the Red Lion and presumably beaten, as the mob took pity on the hangman. Talk began to fill the inn about how this was no accident. It was only then revealed to Burrows more about the crime that John Connor had committed and that the man who was with Connor at the time of the crime was never found. It was a scary moment for the hangman and a rude awakening for him. What you can do in Chester, you probably shouldn't do when you are somewhere else. Connor, unaware of the commotion from his cell at Ruthin Gaol, would find out in the morning that the execution was still going ahead. If Caddock was working on behalf of Connor in order to prevent his impending death then it had failed. The hangman was still alive ... but only just.

Burrows arose in the morning slightly worse for wear partly due to his hangover but also because of the swelling around his neck from his own noose. He prepared himself in his usual way as a hearty breakfast was busily being prepared for him. Shortly before eleven o'clock, there was a knock at his door. It was time.

The execution itself was different from what Burrows was used to. There would be no lever, no massive audience of thousands to entertain, and no short walk to the gallows. Instead, Burrows sat on the carriage alongside John Connor as the procession left Ruthin Gaol and headed towards Galltegfa, which was about a mile away from the centre of Ruthin. The two men sat in silence as Burrows stared at the man he believed could have been in some way responsible for the actions of the previous night.

Galltegfa had been the traditional place for execution for those convicted in Ruthin and it was also normal for a small crowd to follow the condemned procession as they sat on their own coffin on the back of the carriage. Connor had only one demand and that was that his family and friends back in Wexford knew nothing about his execution and should not be informed about his fate.

For Burrows, it would have been very different from what he was used to and although briefed beforehand he would have gone about his business with the same level of disdain for the prisoner as he usually did. Only this time around, there would be no show complete with his usual display of goading towards the crowd. If anything it was just a professional execution. Nothing more, nothing less.

A traditional gallows would await the men as the carriage arrived at their final destination. Connor then approached the scaffold accompanied by two priests who had been with him the entire morning of his execution. One of them, a Mr Bates, addressed the spectators in the open field. He spoke of Connor's contrition and gave a firm warning to others of the repercussions of crimes such as this. Burrows needed a stool of his own to stand up on in order to place the noose around

Connor's neck. As Mr Bates completed his short speech, all Burrows now needed to do was to kick the stool on which Connor was standing and then watch as the slow strangulation took place. The newspapers stated that: 'He was turned off about twenty minutes before one, and died in about two minutes and a half.'[7]

All that remained was to cut Connor down once his last breath and final convolution had passed. Burrows would have then placed John Connor into the coffin that had accompanied them on their journey. With no family to claim his body as was the custom for any condemned criminal other than murderers, it would be up to the parish to bury Connor.

With his job complete Burrows headed back to Chester. It had been a strange experience for him but if anyone believed that his near-death experience would see any lasting change in his demeanour then they would be sorely mistaken. Once back in the safety of Chester, Burrows swiftly returned to his usual ways. Only this time, at least, he had a great story to tell, one about how the hangman went to Ruthin and very nearly, never came back.

Chapter 11

Five Days Racing and a Hanging

The Executions of William Tongue and George Groom
New City Gaol, Chester, 1822

FRESH FROM HIS exploits in Ruthin, Burrows returned to Chester. The timing worked out perfectly for him as within days of his return he would be busy preparing for a double execution back in the relative safety of his city. While a double execution also meant a double payday, for someone like Burrows it would also come at one of Chester's busiest periods.

The double execution would take place just days before the May meeting at the Roodee racecourse. The city was heaving with people from all around the county and further afield as they braced themselves for one of the biggest meetings on the horse racing calendar. Punters, jockeys, trainers and even owners strode around the city in the same way as many others, hoping that the races would bring with them new-found riches from the bookmakers. As always, the city was on high alert and where there was wealth on display, there would also be those looking to steal from those who displayed it.

Pickpockets from all around the surrounding area would also descend on Chester hoping to make some easy money as the city was decorated with decadence and the wealth that went with it. The races were always a perfect opportunity to strike as the inebriated higher classes approached the same paths as the Georgian underworld. The pickpockets were not alone as others also made the most of the race meeting.

Bawdy houses would spring up as if from nowhere and were quickly established for a few days in order to offer sexual favours to the more established middle classes and wealthier clientele. Madams would approach houses in Chester offering extra rent and a small percentage of the takings in exchange for allowing their girls to work there. While some would display their moral outrage at such a proposition, others were more than happy to receive the additional income. There were, of course, repercussions to anyone running a bawdy house if caught but the underworld knew how best to keep quiet about such matters. However, in some cases, those caught could easily face the punishment of twelve months of hard labour, as was the case with Joseph Allames who ran one but was caught in 1824.[1] Either way, the deterrent did not outweigh the potential income that quickly came their way.

It was not just prostitution that was in a position to thrive during a week-long race meeting. The hotels and inns were full to the rafters, with some inns opting to host cock fights when the racing was taking place. For the price of 5 shillings, anyone could attend numerous places around Chester to witness the spectacle and, if they wanted to, place a wager or two. The city had become a place of loose morals with a blend of those intoxicated, highly sexed, and easy with their money as the streets became a den of iniquity at every glance. Needless to say, Samuel Burrows loved it.

Knowing that these people were in town for a week made the upcoming execution all the more important for him. With many faces who did know him personally, it gave him the opportunity to wander the streets with even more self-gratification. These were people who would listen to his every word, even as his stories grew even more over-exaggerated than usual. His near-death experience in Ruthin would be undoubtedly one they would all want to hear. Yet Burrows had yet another reason to look forward to the upcoming festivities and prize fighting.

He had heard that Peter Crawley[2] was coming to Chester with a prize fight due to take place at the Cockpit near the Newgate. While it was on strictly need-to-know terms in case the yeomanry decided to break up the fight, the locals knew that with everything going on in the city the likelihood of authorities stopping it would be slim as their attention would be elsewhere. However, before the opportunity to witness Crawley in action for himself, Burrows had some work to do.

While Burrows was away in Ruthin, the Assizes had gathered at Chester Castle. The subsequent Assize had condemned two men to hang upon Burrows' return to Chester. During the trials that took place while Burrows was away, the Assizes had condemned twenty-nine individuals to death. It was a record number for the Chester Assizes and the fact that only two would eventually face the ultimate sanction reminded Burrows of the pitfalls of his profession. Twenty-six had had their sentences reduced to transportation and the appeal of James Lowndes was still being heard. Lowndes was convicted of stealing from a dwelling house and was due to face Burrows, but at the last moment he escaped death and was sentenced to transportation as a life sentence.

That only left William Tongue and George Groom to eventually face Burrows' noose. Yet another one had slipped through the hangman's grasp and the situation was becoming all more frustrating for Burrows. However, two men nearly became just one, only this time it would not be the judges who defied Samuel.

The men would spend two weeks in Chester Castle Gaol prior to their execution, which was scheduled to occur just before the start of the race meeting. It gave George Groom some time to plan his escape. Groom was found guilty of the assault and highway robbery of James Kennerley. Kennerley, an old and infirm man, was found severely beaten but alive. Eight pence was stolen from him and while the amount of money stolen did not warrant a death sentence, it was the severity of the assault that did.[3] Languishing in his cell, Groom made an extraordinary attempt to escape. Using flags tied around his hands, he aimed to leave the gaol through the horizontal flue that helped to heat the gaol. While he succeeded in entering the flue, the sheer heat that he experienced made him turn back to his cell.[4]

With his escape plan thwarted, Groom would face Burrows alongside William Tongue, who was convicted of raping Ann Cope, who was only

9 years old at the time of her ordeal. The full details of Tongue's horrific crime were deemed too sensitive for publication within the Chester newspapers. This in itself was a rare act from the press, who had previously printed cases in full as they were ongoing and at the time of execution. In some cases, the local press were more than happy to publish full details of murder cases and yet they had made the editorial decision to limit what they printed with regards to Tongue.[5]

Perhaps given the possible hatred towards Tongue and the crime that he committed, the authorities of Chester had opted not to publicly parade the two men through the streets of Chester prior to their execution. Instead, they were moved from Chester Castle Gaol to the New City Gaol at five o'clock in the morning as the city was just beginning to awaken. As usual, they were exchanged at the Gloverstone but this time they were placed in a covered cart before heading on the shortest possible route to their condemned cells at New City Gaol. It was a move that was welcomed by the *Chester Courant*, which wrote:

> We highly approve of the alteration; it is praiseworthy and humane, as it affords to the culprits a few hours of uninterrupted devotion, without having their minds distracted, and their feelings agitated by a public procession through the streets. Let us hope, for the sake of humanity, that the practice will be continued on future similar occasions.

When Burrows arrived at the New City Gaol he swiftly went to work. As the two men were receiving the sacrament, Burrows was preparing in his usual manner. It had been a job and a place that he had become so used to that everything was like second nature to him. As he stood on top of the gaol he saw the crowds begin to swell. Some were confused as the traditional parade of the convicts was abandoned; others, in the city for the first time, were simply following the horde and jostling for position to get a better view. As Burrows looked on he realised just how different everything was from the previous and what felt like a more intimate execution in Ruthin.

Five Days Racing and a Hanging

Groom died almost instantly as he fell from the gallows. A larger, more stout man than average, the force of gravity pulled him down quicker and in doing so helped to break his neck and severed the jugular. Tongue, on the other hand, struggled and convulsed in front of the multitude. With each convulsion, the crowd below Burrows cheered urging him to struggle even longer. They were cheering for him to suffer. They wanted it as, given his crime and the fact that the press were not telling them everything, they were imagining the worst case they could think of. When he finally remained still after nearly three minutes, the crowd slowly began to disperse back from where they had come.[6]

For the strangers who found themselves in Chester for a week's racing and cavorting that was coming their way, it was a grim reminder as to where they were. Yet with a week filled with some more illegal activity in mind, the pickpockets and others within the criminal underworld of the Cestrian streets remained undisturbed.

Receiving his pay for the double execution of Tongue and Groom, Burrows felt flush. It could not have come at a better time. After all, when the races are on and the city is booming, there is plenty to keep a man with some money in his pocket entertained for a week of unrelenting pleasures. How much Mary saw of her husband that particular week would be anyone's guess as the inns and hotels of Chester continued to fill.

Chapter 12

On the Road Again

The Execution of Lewis Owen
Carnarvon Gaol, September 1822

THE CALL HAD come for Samuel Burrows to travel again but the timing could not have been worse for his family. His son, Charles, had been getting into minor trouble around Chester but this time around what he had done was more serious than his previous misdemeanours. Charles was now incarcerated in the cells of Chester Castle, much to Samuel's embarrassment.[1] The son of the hangman was now at the mercy of the Assizes and would remain there until his trial. While Mary begged for Samuel to use his influence as the city's hangman to try to help their son, Burrows was swiftly called into duty and told to travel to Carnarvon in order to execute Lewis Owen.

As he waited for his coach at the White Lion Hotel just opposite the Exchange, he braced himself for the long journey with a soothing ale. As he stared at his drink he began to think about Charles in his cell at the Castle. For a man who believed in the power of the judiciary of the country, and who indeed profited from the process as being the finisher of the law, he knew that the likelihood of Charles being pardoned was extremely high. Even though he had tried to explain this to Mary on multiple occasions as so many convicts had previously slipped through his fingers, her maternal instincts were heightened with the threat to her youngest son's well-being.

Burrows began to think that a stint in the Castle was possibly the best thing for Charles. Perhaps it would scare him straight and both Samuel and Mary might start to see a change in his behaviour. His youngest son was arrested for stealing two ducks alongside Robert Evans in the township of Burton, which had all the hallmarks of being some childish prank yet Samuel believed that he would receive some sort of punishment.

With some time remaining, he got himself another drink and began to think about his upcoming trip to Wales. His previous trip across the border had almost killed him due to his drunken antics and with this thought still languishing in his head, Burrows began to ease up on his drinking inside the White Lion. It was probably best to handle this execution with more sobriety than he was used to. Either way, he had plenty to keep his mind occupied on the journey.

Carnarvon had not seen a public execution for almost twenty years as the town geared up to install the gallows. Although Burrows did not know it at the time as his coach arrived, Carnarvon was not in a buoyant mood ahead of his entrance into the town. The execution of Lewis Owen was a fiercely contested moment in the town's history.

Owen was convicted at the Carnarvon Assizes for the shooting of an excise officer during a robbery in Rhyl. Despite being a capital crime, the local authorities did all that they could to spare him the noose. It was claimed that Owen 'laboured under "temporary insanity" when committing the crime thanks to a recent blow on the head by a plank'. Claims were also made that the impending execution was not in the public's interest with it being so long since the town had last witnessed the horror of the gallows. The county's High Sheriff, William Lloyd Caldecot, even wrote to the Home Secretary with his concerns about the impending execution.

Caldecot informed Henry Addington that: 'The trial had already created a sensation, equal to its effects, to that generally intended and supposed to be produced by execution ... I cannot endure the thought of having a human being executed during the time that I am in office.'[2] Despite the pleas of Caldecot, the Home Secretary declined the petition of mercy. The execution would take place and Samuel Burrows would be summoned to carry it out.

Burrows had got the job purely by default. Given the ill feeling towards the planned execution of Lewis Owen, getting an executioner prepared to complete the task was proving to be a difficult task. With this in mind, and following the successful execution of John Connor in Ruthin, the authorities had to write to Chester in order to gain Burrows' services. Yet getting an executioner was not the only issue that the authorities of Carnarvon had to endure.

Such was the feeling within the area, carpenters could not be sourced locally to build the gallows. The gallows were therefore built in Pwllheli and transported to Carnarvon, where they were brought to Morfa Seiont in the dead of night. With the gallows built, the authorities received their second blow as no one in the town would erect it. The High Sheriff, who was so vehemently opposed to the execution, had to employ his own servants to erect the gallows.[3] Even obtaining a cart to transport Owen to his final destination from gaol was proving elusive. Once again, no one wanted to help for fear of being ostracised within the community. In the end, one was bought from an innkeeper and painted black.

When Burrows finally arrived in Carnarvon he was warned not to reveal the purpose of his visit. The grave situation was explained to him and with thoughts of Ruthin still ingrained in his head, Burrows was certainly not going to argue with anyone given the situation. He retired to his room for the night, where he remained until the morning. Knowing the situation that he found himself in, he was already looking forward to returning back to the relative safety of Chester.

The printers were as always quick to make some much-needed income and they knew the execution of Lewis Owen would bring to them. Unlike the broadsides that detailed every aspect of the crime committed by Owen, the printers in Wales opted for something a little different. A four-page booklet was swiftly prepared for this occasion and told the story of Owen's fate in poetic verse.

The poet described the crime that Owen had committed in a lyrical manner but was also keen to stress the enormity of the young man's impending fate. Written in the country's native tongue, it reveals how Owen shot at Mr Sturdy twice during the robbery and left the supervisor for dead before being captured and imprisoned in Ruthin. Transported to Carnarvon for his trial, Owen would face his accuser, who was alive and well. In court, he would recount his story about the fateful night in question.

The poem reveals the attitude of the court that particular day, and indeed the judge himself, saying that:

> And the judge who reported in the name of the three and one,
> Saying, through great excitement, the man must be condemned
> To suffer death on a gallows between white heaven and floor,
> Near the town of Caernarfon, a land of dawn violins.[4]

It also revealed more about Owen's character. A man who had previously served in the military who returned from duty a somewhat changed man who had vices and who had turned away from his righteous path towards the path of Satan. A certain level of doubt must be reserved for any form of a recounting of his tale in this manner but in it the booklet claims to report Owen's final words:

> My pleasure in my life was to follow the lusts of the flesh,
> And deceive young women to suffer reproach and ridicule:
> And my church on Holy Sunday, obediently we will do it
> Which is to get drunk in pubs from morning to afternoon.[5]

A man driven by prostitution and hard liquor who slowly descended into the sins of the world following his return from service. Regardless of which, Burrows would never have known the full reasons for which the condemned stood before him. His sympathy for the condemned never lasted too long, especially when he was so far away from home.

✦ ✦ ✦

Samuel awoke in the morning with his work firmly away from his mind. He felt powerless to help Charles, who was about to face his own trial in Chester. He gave out a sigh and then stretched his muscles in preparation for what he was about to do. He had heard about Owen's attempted murder of Mr Sturdy following his robbery the night before and was left with some comfort that his son was not facing the probability of execution himself. But he knew that a life of criminality was a slippery slope and one that he hoped his son could stay away from. When breakfast arrived, Burrows feasted as if he had not been fed for a while. He knew that he needed his strength today and aimed to leave town as soon as the job was done.

As Lewis Owen boarded the black coach he could hear the sobs from his mother as she escorted him towards the gallows. Burrows was also with him as the procession left the gaol and ascended up towards Morfa Seiont. It was unlike anything Burrows had previously experienced as the procession was all but silent. The sombre atmosphere was only broken by the sound of grief as Owen approached the noose that would eventually end his life. Respectfully, Burrows sensed the mood of the crowd and remained dignified in his work as Owen addressed the crowd in Welsh. Not knowing what was being said, Burrows remained solemn, gazing at the crowd's faces in order to get a sense of the meaning. He then placed the noose over Owen's now hooded head. More cries were heard as Burrows went about his business before eventually dropping the young man.

Reports stated that Owen's mother fainted at the moment her son died. Fearing reprisals from the already unhappy multitude of approximately 12,000 that had gathered to watch the execution, William Lloyd Caldecot brought her to his carriage and took her away to grieve in private. Such was the communal feeling towards the execution itself, Burrows opted to get out of town as quickly as he could as he cut down Owen's lifeless body in haste.[6]

If Burrows believed that he would escape quickly then he was very much mistaken. Boarding a mail coach destined for his hometown, he was spotted by some who had attended the execution and was immediately recognised.⁷ Rather than travel along with Burrows, the crowd that had gathered quickly turned on the stagecoach driver, who in turn threw Burrows out of his coach in order to please the other passengers. Samuel now found himself alone in a strange town that clearly did not want him around.

Knowing that he would have to find another way home, Burrows opted to walk towards the next town in order to simply escape from the situation he had found himself in. Only this time around, it was not due to his showboating. Either way, the walk allowed him to think about things. Soon his mind began to wander to his family. He wondered how Charles might fare with a stint in Chester Castle and, more importantly, how the rest of Chester would view the boy's father.

Chapter 13

Dead Man's Clothes

The Execution of Samuel Fallows
New City Gaol, Chester, 1823

BURROWS WAS A busy man. He had been the city's executioner for twelve years and in that time he had executed thirty-three individuals at the New City Gaol. Fresh from his trips to Ruthin and Carnarvon following the executions of John Connor and Lewis Owen, he was in high spirits. Not only was work plentiful but it was also coming from further afield. In Burrows' mind, he was a man in demand.

Not only was there plenty of work in terms of the gallows that he oversaw but there was also the opportunity to make even more money by selling grim memorabilia from those he executed. As the hangman of Chester, he not only received his retainer for his services and his price for every condemned criminal he hanged, but he was also able to keep certain items from the execution itself. One grisly perk was to keep the nooses and even the clothing worn by those who were sent to eternity following their fateful encounter with Burrows.[1]

The question Burrows faced was what to do with these macabre pieces that were now slowly filling his Northgate Street home. If the condemned were the same size as Burrows, then he could always keep those clothes for himself. However, even more money could be made if he could find people who wanted to buy these items. There were plenty of collectors out there, those who sold broadsides and ballads on the day of the executions themselves would vouch for that.

The busy hub of Northgate Street would give Burrows plenty of opportunities to sell his grizzly wares. Hawking the streets with his noose in hand gave Burrows a lucrative side hustle and one that he was thankful for. But when it came to the execution of Samuel Fallows, Burrows would walk away without his bonus and it was a bitter pill for the hangman to swallow.

Burrows would have met Fallows moments before he was due to execute him at what was now becoming known as 'Sammy's Castle'. Fallows knew full well what he was doing. He was aware that Burrows' bonus was nothing unique to him personally. The leftovers of the gallows were the same bonus for every hangman within the kingdom.

Burrows would have been busy eyeing up Fallows's fine velvets that he wore during his trial and subsequent conviction. He looked like a man with some money behind him, Burrows thought to himself. When Fallows left Chester Castle in order to be exchanged from the county to city boundaries at the Gloverstone, he was still wearing his fine attire from his trial. In Burrows' mind, he was in for a very nice bonus indeed.

What the hangman did not know though was that Fallows was never planning to be executed in the same clothing that he left the Castle in. Instead, he had asked that a more inferior suit should be waiting for him at the New City Gaol. Arriving at the condemned cell within the gaol, he slowly got changed and 'performed this act without any apparent concern'.[2] Burrows would have been incensed when he finally saw him. His bonus was worthless and Fallows knew it. It would be Fallows's final act of defiance as he climbed the creaking wooden steps toward his date with Burrows.

Samuel Fallows had it all. He had secured the tenancy of some farmland from William Davenport of Bramall Hall and his association with the distinguished family gave Fallows the respect and admiration of his neighbours. Despite being in his early 20s, Fallows was climbing the social ladder with relative ease. However, scandal was never too far away from him.

Mary Coups fell pregnant by Fallows. She was a servant girl for the Davenport family at Bramall Hall and the family was very keen for Fallows to do the right thing and marry her. While Fallows agreed in principle, he did so in order to maintain his image among the influential family that had taken him under their wing following the death of his father, who had previously owned the land that the Davenports had now bequeathed him.

Fallows, however, was living a lifestyle of which the Davenports were unaware. With preparations for the wedding in full swing, Fallows announced on the eve of the ceremony that he was unprepared to go through with it. Most of the invited guests only heard that the wedding had been cancelled when they arrived at Bramall Hall eager to celebrate. If this event damaged his reputation within Bramall Hall and the community that surrounded it, then what followed would shock them to their core. Fallows was already with someone else and had been busy wooing Betty Shawcross, 18 miles away in Bredbury.[3]

Fallows' relationship with Betty was a long-established one and had borne him a child three years earlier prior to his affair with Mary Coups. The scandal over the wedding had begun to fade away when the relationship was finally discovered but it would not take long for Fallows to find himself at the centre of the town's attention once more when Betty's body was discovered.

The cause of her death was a single razor slash measuring 5in on the left side of her neck. Severing the jugular vein, her blood streamed across the crime scene. Slashes on her hands suggested that she had put up a fight against her assailant. The razor used remained at the scene. It did not take long for the authorities to go in search of her lover, Samuel Fallows, who had been seen with Betty just before her death.[4]

The White Boar pub in Butterhouse Green was used by the coroner, John Hollins, who was called in to examine Betty's body and any evidence found at the scene. Soon a makeshift court was prepared in the pub as

Hollins aimed to get to the truth before sending the accused to Chester Castle in order to stand before the Assize. Soon, Fallows would have to give testimony in front of Hollins in order to save his own neck.

With no one else implicated, Hollins needed to make the decision as to whether or not he believed Fallows should stand trial. Fallows gave nearly ten hours of his own testimony in front of the inquest jury, who did not believe his alibi. The more he scrambled for answers, the more guilty he looked. The inquest returned a verdict of 'wilful murder' and accordingly Hollins made the necessary arrangements to send Fallows to Chester Castle in order to await his date with the Assize judges for the county.[5]

There was excitement in the air as the crowds gathered outside the Shire Hall on Friday, 11 April 1823 eager to gain a seat for the trial of Samuel Fallows. The trial, which was due to begin at 9am, was set to become the event of the year as the crowd rushed to get any seat they possibly could. The courtroom swelled with 'respectable persons, among whom was a large proportion of elegantly dressed ladies'. The court had never seen an interest like this before as within 'a few minutes, it was filled almost to suffocation'.[6] The situation in court became so dire that even seats reserved for attorneys and clerks were taken up, leading to orders to vacant those seats. Only when the pandemonium was finally cleared did the court allow Samuel Fallows to rise from the holding cell below to attend the bar.

When he ascended, Fallows cut an impressive figure and one that was far detached from that of the more common criminals the court had been so used to seeing in the past. At 24 years of age, he was described as a good-looking man 'of a fair complexion, seemingly 5 feet 10 inches high; was genteelly dressed in a blue coat & trousers, and black waistcoat, with a black handkerchief round his neck'.[7] He stood strongly, looking at the ladies in the crowd, as he announced his plea of not guilty.

Despite his fine attire and his stoic stance against the crime he was accused of, a plethora of witnesses came forward for the prosecution including Captain Salusbury Pryce Humphreys. He was eager to tell the court about Fallows's treatment of Mary Coups, who lived with Captain Humphreys as a servant. He recounted that Coups was pregnant with Fallows' unborn child and despite his promise to marry her claimed that 'his uncle and all relations were all opposed' to the marriage.[8]

Having a witness testify against his character in the form of Captain Humphreys was not a good look for Fallows. Humphreys was not only a well-respected landowner but also possessed an exemplary naval record and served as a magistrate of the county. Just in case members of the jury did not know exactly who he was, he was quick to inform them of his role within the county. His word carried a considerable amount of weight, especially with the amount of circumstantial evidence that followed.

Mary Twedale found the body of Betty Shawcross and described what she saw in considerable detail, while Robert Thorneley recalled seeing Fallows visiting the victim at the home of Mrs Murrey where Shawcross lived.

Rebecca Leigh informed the court that Betty Shawcross wrote a letter intended for Fallows. It was her task to deliver it to The Plough public house, which Fallows frequented regularly. The letter was handed to the landlady, Ann Hickman, who duly delivered it to Fallows when he arrived. Hickman gave the court a full description of what he wore when he received the letter from Shawcross. She said that he was wearing a 'black coat and waistcoat, light small clothes and leggings of a light colour. It was the same dress as he usually wore.' Hickman claimed that Fallows read the letter in her presence and when she asked him if there was a message to be returned, he replied no. The contents of the letter were never revealed.[9]

While it was clear that an affair was going on between the two, evidence concerning his whereabouts at the time of the crime was still nowhere to be seen.

John Walton came forward as witness number nine. Walton was Fallows' servant and slept in the same room as him. He claimed that he went to bed at nine o'clock that night but did not see his master. When Walton awoke at 5 o'clock the next morning, Fallows was still nowhere to be seen. Walton recalled what Fallows had worn the previous day and it was exactly as Hickman had previously described. Then Walton had seen Fallows heading up the road towards Bramall Green, which led him to Shawcross. Seeing his master at twelve o'clock the next day, he informed the court that his clothing had changed. The breaches he wore that day were different and he claimed that he had never seen him wear them before.[10]

Throughout the proceedings, Fallows remained confident. The case against him was largely circumstantial with nothing to directly pin the murder of Betty Shawcross on him. Even the evidence surrounding the razor that was used as the murder weapon could not definitely prove that it was his but the assumption was strong, particularly in the eyes of the judge. In summing up the evidence following an all-day trial, Chief Justice Warren stated that:

> As to the fatal instrument by which the mortal wound was inflicted, if not traced directly to be the property of the prisoner, it cannot be otherwise accounted for, than upon this presumption.[11]

Chief Justice Warren continued with his summing up, highlighting nine key points from the witnesses. In summary, he highlighted the suspicions raised about Fallows's character and his whereabouts during the night in question. While the circumstantial evidence was strong, and Fallows conducted himself in a suspicious manner, it would ultimately be up to the jury to decide Fallows's fate.

The jury deliberated for twenty-six minutes. When asked for their verdict the foreman replied with the cutting word of 'guilty'. The court was silent as Fallows himself remained stunned. While Chief Justice Warren spoke directly to the prisoner, Fallows simply stared ahead of him not quite taking the whole situation in. On passing the sentence of death, Warren highlighted how Fallows had 'seduced the young woman, and killed at once the mother and the child'.[12]

Warren continued, 'Let me, however, remind you, that Monday next will be the last day you will behold the light of the sun. Repent earnestly of your great offence, seek grace and forgiveness without delay, and may heaven grant mercy upon you.'[13]

Samuel Burrows was on duty at Chester Castle Gaol as Samuel Fallows was guided back to his cell. Watching the handsome Fallows glide past him, Burrows was immediately drawn to his clothes. The hangman was duly informed that the execution would take place on Monday, giving the prisoner three more evenings to prepare his soul. As he was being spoken to about the imminent execution, Burrows already knew that Fallows's clothes would not fit him personally but he could easily sell them to an interested buyer.

With little time to prepare, an excited Burrows left the gaol in a hurry, returning to Northgate Street to tell Mary about their latest payday. While Samuel was delighted, the same could not be said for Mary. She was still grieving for her son Henry, who had died in the East Indies while serving in the British Army alongside Lord Cumbermere. It was a grief so fierce that it had consumed her. She blamed Samuel for encouraging Henry to join the subdivision of the Hundred of Broxton by recalling his own stories of conflict. It was a conversation that often led to arguments and the situation was made even worse as their youngest son, Charles, was getting into even more trouble.

At this particular moment in time, Samuel knew that Mary was having one of those days when her grief overwhelmed her. Samuel grieved too for the death of his eldest son but he opted to find other ways to numb the pain. Rather than facing another argument, Burrows left and headed to the public houses, not only to drink away his thoughts but also with the aim of finding a potential buyer for Samuel Fallows's clothes.

Dead Man's Clothes

Fallows awoke on his final morning at four o'clock. An attempt to bribe his way out of the Castle and escape the noose had failed. The previous day, it was reported that Fallows had offered bribes of up to £1,000 in order to help him escape. The *Chronicle* stated that 'a person evidently acquainted with the Prisoner' had approached a senior warder with the promise of payment.[14]

The city authorities had previously recommended that the usual procession route through the streets of Chester should be altered. Now, in the early hours of the morning, the condemned criminals due for execution would take a shorter route directly down Nicholas Street before turning left towards the New City Gaol. The news was a disaster for those who had established a livelihood based around the excitement of public executions as the early hour meant the crowd was scheduled to miss the parade.

Fallows left Chester Castle Gaol via the debtors' door and embarked on his final short journey under the relative cover of darkness as the city began to wake. Despite being so early, 'a vast concourse of people had assembled to witness the mournful procession'. If the authorities had hoped that the macabre procession that the city had grown accustomed to would be scarcely spectated, then they were very much mistaken. Waiting for him at New City Gaol were his brother and sister, who had arranged to meet him there.[15]

His siblings had brought with them what Fallows requested. Despite wearing his fine attire while confined to Chester Castle, he had urged them to bring the ragged clothes that he decided to wear at his execution. Now changed and after spending his last moments with his loved ones, Fallows spent an hour with the gaol's chaplain. Reverend Ayckbown administered the holy sacrament before an excited Burrows arrived to pinion the condemned man.[16]

As the door opened, Fallows stared at Burrows. He knew exactly what he had done. Before Burrows was a man in rags and far from the fine gentleman who he had witnessed at Chester Castle. Burrows, trying to hide his disdain for the condemned in front of those who surrounded him, pinioned Fallows with a little more force than was required. Burrows felt sick knowing that his bonus was all but worthless to him.

Leaving to entertain the masses, Burrows was furious. There would be no show today, instead, he went about his business with a firm focus and desire to get the job done. Hiding his feelings was almost impossible. The amassed crowd looked confused, mumbling to one another about Burrows' demeanour.

Even as Fallows ascended the gallows, Reverend Ayckbown was still attempting to save his soul, yet the man who now stood on top of the New City Gaol shrugged him away. Fallows remained steadfast in his desire not to show any fear as Burrows fastened the noose. However, no matter how still he remained, it could not last as Burrows released the mechanism sending Fallows beneath him.[17]

For three minutes, Fallows struggled as he hung before the Chester crowd. Burrows watched his rope sway before him as Fallows' futile fight for life continued. He was not thinking about cutting him down and delivering his body to the surgeons, all that he was thinking about was how he was going to explain to his buyer that the fine clothes that he had promised to deliver were now no longer in his possession.

Chapter 14

The Changing Tide

The Execution of John Kragon
New City Gaol, Chester, 1823

AS SAMUEL BURROWS glanced at the *Chester Courant* on 15 April 1823 he must have believed that he was in for a bumper payday. He mainly bought a copy for its long write-up about the trial and execution of Samuel Fallows but he was dismayed not to see his name in print. However, something else had also grabbed his attention for he knew that it would not be long until he was on the scaffold again.

As he scanned the front page he could see how many death sentences were passed at the Assizes. From it, he could begin to calculate exactly how busy he could be. He read the names and their eventual sentences without much concern for their actual crimes. All he was interested in was how much pay he could expect to receive.

Glancing through he read them all one by one. John Booth, Guilty, John Smith, Guilty.

Already, Burrows knew that those names were worthless to him. They would probably get some kind of custodial sentence or a period of hard labour. Nevertheless, he continued to scan the news. William Williamson, seven years' transportation, Edward Jones, twelve months of hard labour in the house of correction. Then finally came the news Burrows was most interested in.[1]

John Wakefield, death. Francis Nuttall, William Cheetham, and Jacob Barber, death. John Kragon, death. Burrows' eyes lit up. Five would mean an excellent payday indeed. Yet of the five, only one would potentially face Burrows's noose. Wakefield, Nuttal, Cheetham, and Barber would all later receive more lenient sentences following their successful appeals for mercy from the judges.[2] Kragon had also submitted a petition for mercy to the Crown, where his fate was now resting with the Home Secretary, Robert Peel. It would be an anxious wait for both Kragon and his restless hangman, who had already seen many slip through his grasp.

Kragon's crime sent shockwaves throughout the Assizes when it finally came to trial. While some of the evidence was deemed too horrific to publish, the *Chester Courant* was more than happy to give some details of the case that was now sitting on Peel's desk in Westminster. Within the space of a week, Kragon would know the Home Secretary's response.

Jemima Ward was only 8 years old at the time of Kragon's attack on her. She worked at a factory in Porton. Like many her age, she was of vital importance to a family's survival as she scurried underneath the factory looms to gather the dropped cotton on the floor. According to her father, Jemima 'was in the habit of returning from her work about 8 or half past 8 o'clock at night'. Mr Ward could almost time his watch by her return but on the night in question, Jemima was late. Needless to say, he had begun to think that the worst may have happened to his daughter. When she did finally return, he breathed a sigh of relief but it was her stepmother, Sarah Ward, who noticed that something was not quite right. The *Courant* reported that Sarah had 'observed that she walked lame, but could not get her to acknowledge what ailed her for a fortnight afterwards'.[3]

Finally, Jemima began to talk to Sarah about her ordeal. Jemima knew of John Kragon but never by his name. Instead, she knew him purely by sight. She had seen him many times around the market and knew him as the man who carried potatoes based largely on his much disfigured right eye. It would be this disfigurement that she would recognise once again late one night in November as she walked home from the factory.

Kragon overtook her and as he turned around and faced Jemima she was able to see his right eye due to the light that came from a shop window. Frozen with fear, Jemima remained still as Kragon asked: 'Little girl, will you come with me?'

Jemima, in fear for her own safety, replied: 'No, I must go home.'[4]

It was not the answer that Kragon wanted to hear. He grabbed the young girl by her arm and 'forced her with him up the brow into an entry opposite the High-Street school, and there effected his purpose'. It was a savage rape that the *Courant* was reluctant to go into detail about. Kragon aimed to keep his young victim silent about the crime by telling her that if the news should ever get out then they both would hang. It was a threat that kept her quiet for two weeks before she finally opened up to her stepmother.[5]

The 21-year-old Kragon swiftly found himself arrested following Jemima's evidence to the authorities. Following a brief inquest he was sent to Chester Castle to await his case hearing at the Assizes. Throughout his trial, he claimed his innocence and aimed to prove this with an alibi in the form of Edward O'Donnel, who kept a lodging house in Manchester. O'Donnel stated that 'from the first of November to the 21st he (Kragon) was never out of his lodgings a single night later than half-past nine'. It implied that it would be impossible for Kragon to get back to his lodgings in time but the court did not deem his evidence satisfactory.

The jury did not believe a word from Kragon and sided with the prosecution. Found guilty of rape, the Chief Justice reminded the court about the case of William Tongue and stated that he had hoped that execution would 'deter others from the commission of such crimes in future'. With Tongue executed for a similar crime, Kragon received the same sentence of death.[6]

A distraught Kragon left the court continuing to plead his innocence but it fell on deaf ears. Now his only hope for a lighter sentence depended on the Home Secretary, who it was believed favoured sentences other than death in the most serious of cases.

The mayor, William Massey, sent off Kragon's plea for mercy and awaited a response. As his petition was being heard, Kragon remained in Chester Castle with a faint belief that his life could be spared in favour of transportation. Once the petition was sent, he was given a respite of fourteen days regardless of the eventual outcome.

Burrows was far from happy to hear that a man like Kragon might potentially slip through his grasp. It was becoming all too frequent and he was beginning to feel that his very livelihood was at stake. For Robert Peel though, Burrows had a particular disdain. Peel had already been vocal about his views on the 'Bloody Code' earlier in his career and now Burrows' arch nemesis held the esteemed office of Home Secretary.

Arguments against the Bloody Code were something that the country was becoming all too used to. Reformers had come and gone but in Peel, executioners around the kingdom had a more formidable foe. Even before Peel came on to the scene, reformers such as Sir William Meredeith and Sir Samuel Romilly had tried but failed to change the laws of the land with regard to the Bloody Code. However, their work was not in vain. A discussion about the severity of the law was now firmly established, with Peel and his allies now in a prime position to make the repeals stick.[7]

Following Sir Samuel's death in 1818, Sir James Mackintosh took up the mantle with more vigour. While some of his proposals might have fallen on deaf ears, Mackintosh continued his fight by adding a further nine proposals on 21 May 1823. His aim was to reduce the punishment for smaller crimes to either custodial sentences or to amend potential death sentences in favour of transportation to the colonies.[8]

Robert Peel was listening intently to the arguments. He became the Home Secretary in 1822 with the aim of amending the criminal codes throughout the United Kingdom. Peel aimed to reform the entire system from gaols, prisoner reform, education and the introduction of payment to gaolers from central sources rather than being paid by the inmates. Corruption within the gaol system was rife and the need to bring it into line was of paramount importance to Peel. He also believed that the prison system was overcrowded due mainly to the number of crimes that the Bloody Code deemed as capital crimes that resulted in a death sentence. With Peel and the likes of Mackintosh and others becoming kindred spirits with regard to the reform of the Bloody Code, Burrows firmly believed that his livelihood would become seriously affected. But for now, the only thing that mattered to Burrows was the fate of Kragon.

The Changing Tide

The summons for Burrows to meet with Mayor Massey had finally arrived. Burrows prepared himself and then walked quickly towards the Exchange. It was a purposeful walk as his very presence made others move out of his way. He wanted Kragon gone, not only because of the crime that he had committed but also because he knew that there was a likelihood that he might get a more lenient sentence. As he stormed up the stairs Massey was waiting for him.

Massey revealed the contents of the letter sent by Robert Peel with regards to Kragon. Peel had submitted the petition to Mr Justice Warren rather than decide himself. For now, Peel was letting the law decide. Warren, after making further inquiries, believed that in this case Kragon should hang for his hideous crime. Burrows was told to prepare himself and get everything in place for Saturday as Kragon still had a few days left of his petition for mercy remaining in order to prepare himself.

Burrows was ecstatic. In his mind justice could be served and, more importantly, he would be paid. He went straight to the New City Gaol to prepare and alerted the scaffolders to erect the gallows. With his buoyant mood still intact, he quickly made his way back to Northgate Street in the knowledge that some premises frequently provided him with credit when an upcoming execution was approaching. As he drank he began to spread the word about Saturday's execution. Eventually nearly everyone in the city knew Kragon's fate, except the man himself. He was still languishing in his cell clinging to the faint hope of leniency.

The Kragon case represents a key turning point for Burrows and executioners around the country. The tide was changing but, unknown to them, there were moves in Westminster that could see their own profession change completely. As Burrows stood on top of the New City Gaol with Kragon, he had no idea that things were about to get worse for him. Kragon's execution in Chester would be the last under the current laws of the land.

Burrows was summoned to meet the mayor again a month later, only this time it seemed strange to the hangman as he knew that there were no upcoming executions. He began to think about what the mayor could possibly want from him. A flogging might be needed at the gaols but that was doubtful as this time around a specific date for the meeting was mentioned so it could not be that. Something else must have happened, he thought to himself.

In the days as he waited for his meeting, Burrows began to drink more frequently. He was all too aware of Peel's new motion to Parliament that would challenge the Bloody Code in a way that had not been seen before. All Peel and his allies needed was enough votes to make it law. Each time they were inching closer as further amendments were added and Burrows began to think that his own fate would be sealed in London.[9]

As Sammy left his home before his meeting with the mayor, Mary knew all too well where he would head. The Old Woolpack on Shoemakers Row was just south of the Exchange and had become one of his favourite watering holes. George Woolley held the licence and would regularly welcome Burrows in, not only for a drink but also to offer a friendly ear. Not all landlords welcomed Burrows given his previous exploits but Woolley was all too aware that something was not quite right. The pair would have discussed the current situation that the hangman found himself in as Burrows drank more heavily than usual.

Burrows slowly walked up through the crowded street to find out exactly what the new law had said. As he made his way through the horde of market traders and their customers, he knew all too well that life would never be the same again for him.

The Exchange had dominated Northgate Street since 1698. While much work had been done to it since then, the importance of the building could never be understated. Prior to 1756, the ground level of the building was more open and supported by four rows of stone columns. It would be here where traders made their living but the city was growing concerned with the safety of the structure and later redeveloped the lower lever with brick in order to give the building more stability. Some traders were allowed to remain but the rest of the ground level had now become occupied with police offices and a lock-up for anyone who broke the peace of the city.[10]

A new entrance was added on the southern side of the building complete with emblazoned symbolic coats of arms for the City of Chester and the county of Cheshire. In the centre of the coat of arms was a statue of Queen Anne, the monarch who sat at the time of the completion of the building. As Burrows made his way towards her figure he would have seen the stairs complete with their elegant arching entrance. He wouldn't be visiting the shops or chatting with those who manned the lock-up like he used to do back when he was the parish beadle. Instead, he slowly climbed the stairs to face those who governed the city.

Each step felt heavy as Burrows began to think to himself that this must have been how it felt to walk up to his own execution. The only difference was that his particular gallows were not in the open air on top of the New City Gaol in front of a multitude of spectators. Instead, he would be in front of William Massey, the Mayor of Chester, and his Sheriffs, William Davenport and Edward Ducker.[11]

The top floor of the Exchange was where the legislators and elected officials worked. The spacious town hall might have been where the daily rigours of debate and officiating occurred but Burrows was not summoned there. Instead, he was asked to report to the council chamber on the far side of the luxurious assembly room. Each footstep echoed around the hall as he felt the portraits that adorned the wall staring at him with a level of disdain.

When Burrows entered the council chamber he was warmly greeted by Massey. The pair had known each other for a while and while Massey was not particularly impressed with Burrows' antics on the gallows, he also knew that the news he was about to give him would change not only his life but also the frequency of executions in Chester. Even a politician knew that empathy was needed at this particular moment in time. Burrows was offered a drink, sat down, and heard the change in the law in full. Failing to understand it fully, Sheriff Davenport repeated it in a language that Burrows could comprehend.[12]

Burrows was in a daze. He looked around and saw the large portrait of George III behind where Mayor Massey was sitting. He began to sympathise with the former king in respect to his own fate. Slowly ousted just like him, Burrows thought to himself. The world was changing and

Burrows did not like it one bit. Burrows did not want change, he wanted everything to stay exactly as it was.

He left the Exchange crestfallen, filled with anguish and an unrelenting bitterness. With little spare change in his pocket, he opted to head home to break the news to Mary. Entering his home, he asked where Charles was but Mary revealed that their son was out with his friends. Probably up to no good, Burrows thought to himself. Charles had not taken the news of his brother's death well and had recently been hanging around with what Burrows called 'no goods'. He sensed that his youngest was heading down a slippery slope but with himself and Mary in what felt like a constant state of grief, Samuel simply sat back and hoped that Charles would eventually come to some sense. He glanced up at Mary, who naturally asked what was said at the Exchange.

Burrows revealed what he understood of the conversation given all the legal jargon that he had heard.

Essentially, what he took away was that the number of crimes that could now be deemed punishable by death would significantly reduce and that judges could use their discretion to give lesser sentences. Only acts of treason or murder would receive an automatic death sentence. Judges could give a death sentence to some other crimes but the new law meant that he could also commute the sentence to imprisonment or transportation.

Either way, for Burrows it was a bitter pill to swallow. He knew that from this moment his days on top of the New City Gaol would become less frequent and that money would soon be harder to find. All he could do was to hope that the judges at Chester Assizes would at least maintain their hard line and use their discretion wisely enough to keep him employed.

Mary remained silent. She knew all too well that Samuel had a temper. Instead, she allowed him to sit down and take the news in. Any reaction from her would light the touchpaper that would eventually explode the powder keg. Burrows just sat in silence and all that could be heard was the crackling of the fire. More fuel was needed to keep warm but Burrows was in no mood to replenish the dying flames. He was staring at the floor and in his mind he was cursing the likes of Robert Peel and their do-gooding.

He needed to think about his next move, a different way to bring some stability into the household. Another part-time job was needed in order to compensate for the losses that were about to come his way.

Rather than concern himself with a much-needed drink to stem his mood, Burrows began the difficult task of trying to find more work. While he knew that he could gain an extra 5 shillings for dishing out corporal punishment when needed at either of the gaols within the boundaries of Chester, the work was less frequent than he wanted. Something regular was needed.

He went to his old place of work on the Shambles of Northgate Street. As a former butcher, he believed that his skills could still be used, especially as he saw apprentices hacking their way through a carcass with a certain level of ineptitude. Perhaps he could show them how it was meant to be done. He remembered his old work well although he had not entertained the idea of returning to his trade since becoming the city's hangman. As he approached the wooden shacks that made up the butchers on the Shambles he felt the offal and congealed blood beneath his shoes as the cobbles gathered the unsightly and stinking mess. He approached each of his former colleagues asking for some work, all of whom declined. No one wanted to employ a man who sent dozens to their deaths, especially the way Burrows did with so much gusto.

Burrows needed something where he could simply get on with the job at hand, without prying eyes and gossip-makers pecking his ears. It also dawned on him that his previous behaviour on the scaffold in full view of the public had made him a notorious character. It was only then that he spied the local rat-catcher going about his business and followed him to see how he went about his profession. He watched him setting traps, using his dog to gather the scent of the rodents, and then taking rats away to gather his pay. It all seemed simple enough and, more importantly, it was the kind of work that could be done alone. For a hangman practically ostracised from working society, it was perfect. Although his mind was already made up, Samuel headed home in order to tell Mary about his new plan.

Chapter 15

The Curious Case of Charles Burrows

CHARLES BURROWS WAS a troubled lad. The youngest son of the city's hangman had never had the relationship that Samuel enjoyed with his eldest son, Henry. There was a seven-year age difference between the two boys, with Charles born in 1808. Throughout his young life, he would only have known his father to be the hardened hangman of Chester and because of that it would be a strained relationship and one where Charles knew that he was not the favoured son. While Samuel doted on his eldest, the same could not necessarily be said for Charles.

Henry's untimely death while serving in the East Indies had driven a further wedge between the two as both Samuel and Mary grew into a deep depression brought on by their grief. Sammy took to drink even more so than usual following Henry's death, with his behaviour on the gallows becoming more unpredictable. While he always wanted to put on a macabre show for the multitudes who attended his public executions, he now found himself doing so in a more inebriated state and not necessarily through choice as addiction took its firm hold on him.

It must have been a difficult situation for a young Charles, watching his father in this state both around the streets of Chester and also at home. Perhaps it was no wonder Charles's behaviour began to change as he searched for some kind of acceptance away from the drunken chaos of his father and the deep grief of his mother. Needless to say, given the circumstances that he found himself in, the young and susceptible Burrows began to stumble into the world of petty crime.

The Curious Case of Charles Burrows

Samuel later said that Charles was 'a bad lad, and would not keep from evil company',[1] but at the same time he had failed to realise his own part in the making of his own son's behaviour. As the city's executioner, he knew all too well that having a son who was veering towards the realms of criminality would not be looked on too kindly by his own employers. Charles was frequently getting into trouble but was not quite on the radar of the Chester authorities as he was largely committing his petty crimes away from the city itself.

Charles' crimes were not seen as enough to warrant too much punishment in terms of nineteenth-century law. He was convicted of stealing two ducks alongside Robert Evans in the township of Burton in January 1823 but was released soon after.[2] But if Samuel thought that could be enough to scare his wayward son straight then he would be sorely mistaken as his son's name would appear in the papers again in January 1824.

This time Charles was arrested in Wrexham but with little evidence to hold him he was swiftly released from custody. However, this small piece that appeared in the *Chester Chronicle* revealed who Charles' father was. It stated:

> Charles Burrows, son of the Jack Ketch for 'this and the adjacent counties', was apprehended in Wrexham, on a charge of too closely inspecting the pockets of those whom he came in contact with. There not being sufficient evidence to send him to trial, he was discharged.[3]

Samuel would have been incensed as he read the piece. His son's behaviour was becoming more and more dangerous and the reference to Jack Ketch, a common slang term for all hangmen around the country named after the infamous executioner of the fifteenth century, had identified him personally. Yet, according to Burrows himself, there was also an element of fatherly concern. With his son on a path towards more serious criminality, which could eventually lead to execution, Burrows knew that he had to do something in order to save his own son's neck.

William Jones sold stockings. Every Saturday morning, Jones would bring his stall to the city, quietly set his stall up, and prepare for what he hoped would be a lucrative day on the streets of Chester. He had firmly established himself among other traders within Eastgate Street as his voice boomed through the area highlighting his latest stock. Keeping an eye on the stall as people came and went was Charles Burrows and some of his friends. As they admired the contents of the stall, they certainly had no intention of paying for the goods that they fancied.

Yet Jones was a wily old tradesman. He was always on constant alert for any potential thieves and had developed a method of selling while also remaining vigilant. He spotted Charles stalking his stall, walking back and forth waiting for his opportunity to pinch whatever he could. When Jones' back was turned for a moment, Burrows pounced. However, at the time Jones saw nothing.

It was only when he was checking his stock that Jones realised that he had been robbed as some stockings that he later claimed were not sold that day had now vanished. His thoughts immediately switched to the young man he had seen earlier who stalked his stall suspiciously.

Burrows was later apprehended by the city watchman, John Ryley, who searched him. Ryley found the missing stockings under Charles's hat and inside his jacket pocket. It was enough to lock him away.[4] Samuel would later claim that he was in some way involved in the apprehension of his own son. He stated clearly that, 'I was the means for sending him off, for I could not screen such evils, for it would be the greatest injustice to mankind.'[5]

Despite Samuel's claims, he did not appear on any official record with regard to his own involvement in Charles's subsequent arrest. Perhaps he tipped off John Ryley as to his son's whereabouts or maybe he had asked him to keep a close eye on him? Whether Charles knew about his father's involvement in his apprehension is unclear and maybe Samuel even kept this knowledge away from his own wife. Either way, Charles was caught.

Charles was placed into the very same gaol where his own father unashamedly executed the criminals who were condemned to hang. Burrows' 16-year-old son was now awaiting his own trial at the Assizes at Chester Castle. Only a year earlier, Charles would have been facing the prospect of a potential execution himself to be carried out by his own father but with the recent changes to the law and the introduction of the Judgement of Death Act that had seen Samuel's role diminish, it would also be the act that would save his son's life. Charles was incarcerated until his trial date at the city sessions.

He would be found guilty at the city sessions on 10 April 1824. It was news that the young Burrows did not take well. Enraged by the verdict and his sentence of seven years' transportation to the colonies, Charles went on to bad mouth everyone involved and damned them all to hell. He claimed that he never stole the stockings but knew who did and would never reveal that particular information.[6]

Charles was later transported to a prison hulk ship, where he would stay until he could be transported to Van Diemen's Land. He would not be alone. In total, five men that day would be sentenced to the same punishment, all of whom would join Burrows on the long journey by cart from Chester to the Justitia hulk on 4 May 1824. William Jones would join Burrows on the cart for stealing books, as well as Richard Sant, Thomas and James Broomhall. All five were aged between 15 and 23 years old as they made their way towards Woolwich on the docks of the River Thames.[7]

What awaited Charles Burrows shocked him to the core. Far away from the relative quaintness of Chester, he arrived in London to see his first glimpse of what would be his temporary home before his inevitable transportation to Van Diemen's Land. The River Thames was lined with prison hulks used to imprison inmates from all walks of life. With a degree of trepidation, Charles entered the Justitia hulk, which was now permanently moored in the centre of the river, via a small boat that was painstakingly rowed towards the 260-ton hulk that seemed all but impossible to escape from. With the river now acting as a natural moat and heavily guarded both on the hulk itself and on the shoreline, Burrows knew that he was completely trapped.

Unlike Chester Castle, where he was largely surrounded by petty criminals, the hulks represented something entirely new to him. Any safety that he thought he could have expected due to his age quickly evaporated as he now found himself surrounded by some of the country's most hardened criminals. Furthermore, he was expected to work for his bread and board. Each day until his eventual transportation, Burrows would leave the hulk to be taken back to shore, where he would be expected to work on the docks. While his work would vary, it was always hard physical labour from digging canals to building walls. This would become the norm for around ten hours a day before he was taken back to the hulk and chained to the floor to prevent any chance of escape. Compared to his previous incarceration, this was hell on Earth.[8]

Samuel, of course, heard nothing from his son during the duration of his sentence. He had no idea what life was like for his son on board the hulk and the subsequent journey to Van Diemen's Land. An ever-concerned Mary sank into a further depression. In her eyes, she had now lost both her sons. Even though Charles was still alive, she still mourned him as she did Henry. Despite Samuel continuing to attempt to ease his wife's concerns, it fell on deaf ears as the two of them continued with their everyday lives.

Charles survived his two-month stint on the Justitia hulk but it had hardened him. If Mary had seen him following his incarceration on the Justitia, she would barely recognise him as he adapted to his surroundings with relative ease. Charles, although only 16 years old, had become a man and a fearsome one at that.

On 3 July 1824, Burrows boarded the *Princess Charlotte* ahead of his four-month voyage to Van Diemen's Land.[9] He was 1 of 140 convicts who boarded the ship to face the long journey. On board, Charles would have experienced slightly better conditions than that on the hulk. By the time he was transported to the other side of the world, the journey had somewhat improved. Previously, many convicts would have died en route as disease and pestilence took over the boats. The late eighteenth century had seen the worst of the conditions for transported criminals, with around one in ten convicts dying during the journey. However, by the time Charles made his journey, conditions had improved and the mortality rate had reduced significantly.

The *Princess Charlotte* came equipped with a small infirmary and its own surgeon-superintendent, who was responsible for looking after all who boarded the ship. John Dobie was *Princess Charlotte*'s surgeon-superintendent for the journey on which Charles found himself and he kept a meticulous journal, recording everyone who came to him seeking attention.[10]

For Dobie, the line between convict and guard meant nothing. All were entitled to any medical assistance, not only for their own individual well-being but for the wellness of the ship as a whole. Disease was particularly contagious on board ships transporting convicts and any sign of it was monitored closely. Thankfully for Dobie, everyone made the journey with only minor illnesses recorded. Many of the illnesses on board the *Princess Charlotte* amounted to vomiting, diarrhoea, nausea, and pulsating headaches, which were all typical illnesses experienced by those travelling on ships.

Concerned about ongoing vomiting and diarrhoea on board that affected a few convicts, Dobie suggested that the journey should temporarily halt in Rio de Janeiro. Dysentery was a constant fear on board the ship given its ability to spread like wildfire. In order to precaution against the disease, Dobie recommended to the master that *Princess Charlotte* be restocked with fresh beef and vegetables while in Brazil.

Charles Burrows' never appears in Dobie's journal, indicating that he never sought any medical treatment. The hangman's youngest son was 1 of approximately 72,500 British convicts who arrived on the shores of Van Diemen's Land between 1803 and 1853 and, like many who arrived, the newly established town of Hobart would be his home for the foreseeable future.[11] Although he was sentenced to seven years, many convicts would never return to Britain, opting instead to use their freedom to rebuild their lives in either Van Diemen's Land or via a brief trip over water north to New South Wales in Australia.

What exactly happened to Charles Burrows while in Van Diemen's Land is a mystery. Only three documents have survived from his time there. The passenger list shows that he arrived safely. Once on dry land, Burrows entered the Hobart Penitentiary. All convicts received a tick by their name to indicate that they had arrived. Charles was then measured and any identifiable marks were compiled on to the description list.

Standing at 5ft 6in with light brown hair and blue eyes, the 16-year-old Burrows who left Chester in April now claimed that he was 19 years of age. He stated that his occupation was that of a labourer, and he was described as 'much pock pitted' over his face and body. Given his occupation, there is a great likelihood that he would have stayed in Hobart in order to help build the town or worked elsewhere under a guardianship. His release date was stated as 13 April 1831.[12]

Burrows appears to have survived his sentence, unlike some of his fellow inmates. Francis Brooker was sentenced to life on the colony yet in a ghastly postscript it simply states on the record that he was 'murdered by the natives'. John Burk was another unfortunate who, despite being released on 11 August 1830, was later executed in 1835.[13]

The final document focuses on Charles's conduct during his sentence. Compared to many, he appears to have kept his nose relatively clean. He appears twice for somewhat minor misdemeanours. Forming a gang with fellow Cestrian convicts, they refused to turn out for work and were subsequently punished. As part of this gang, he was involved in an incident of 'taking a boat from her moorings'.[14] His transgressions while serving his sentence appear somewhat juvenile in their nature. Charles, it appears at least, either left Van Diemen's Land following his release or remained there and rebuilt his life.

From that point on, Charles vanishes from any official documents. What became of him is unknown. For Samuel Burrows and his wife, the time had come to move from one end of Chester to another. The family home on Northgate Street had served its purpose, although with an ever-dwindling income during the course of the late 1820s, the couple had no choice but to move elsewhere. Packing their few worldly possessions, they looked around their once-busy room. It was a room full of memories, some of love and others of loathing, but either way Mary gazed around with a tear in her eye. Samuel put his arm around her in an attempt to comfort her.

They looked in the corner of the room and smiled at each other. It was here where a young Charles slept, laughed, cried, and played with his brother. Recalling their memories, the pair comforted each other before Mary turned to Samuel with a tear on her cheek. Their boys were now gone and the memories were all they had left to cling to. Now they had to take themselves and their possessions to Brook Street, where cheaper dwellings awaited them.

Chapter 16

The Hangman's Idle Hands

BURROWS DID NOT respond to Robert Peel's reforms to the Bloody Code too well, nor to the fact that Charles was on his way to Van Diemen's Land. In the space of a few months, his world had turned upside down. His primary income was now from rat catching and the dwindling income had forced both Mary and himself to move away from Northgate Street. His old way of life was slowly becoming but a faded memory. The regular executions that he once thrived on were becoming more sporadic and the respect that he foolishly believed his position gave him had all but evaporated.

He now lived in Brook Street, away from the centre of Chester. The Gorse Stacks area of Chester was more industrial than that of Northgate Street and he was surrounded by the cattle market and the local tanneries that thrived in the area.[1] The industries around the canal had also grown but Burrows longed to be back in the centre of the action rather than waking every morning to the smell of the tannery just down the road.

Whether he liked it or not, this was his new home as the number of executions he was asked to perform slowly dwindled. However, it was an ideal location for his other occupation as a rat-catcher as the number of rats grew around the canal making the most of the mills around the area to feed. Burrows was only a short walk away from the centre of the city but in moving to this area he felt as if the importance of his main profession was ebbing away.

Thankfully for Burrows, Brook Street had its own public house in the form of the Cottage Tavern, which was run by John Davies.[2] Burrows would become a frequent visitor. When he entered, the tavern would temporarily fall silent as the tanners, cattlemen and canal workers recognised him. The hangman's notoriety followed him wherever he went but here he did not possess the level of celebrity that he once felt that he had in Northgate Street. Careful of the judgemental eyes that surrounded him, Burrows took a seat and removed his hat. Davies cared little for how Burrows gained his income. For him, the man who sat before him was worth his weight in gold in terms of business. Despite the earlier apprehension of the regulars, Burrows would soon call the place his local.

Yet, the centre of the city was constantly calling to him. It was a place where he felt more alive as the hustle and bustle not only excited him, but it was where he thought he could make the most of his notoriety. His level of self-importance may have swelled his head but in reality he had become a figure to be mocked rather than feared. With little to do, Burrows did not need much persuasion to roam the streets and frequent the public houses, desperately attempting to sell merchandise from previous executions. His life was slowly becoming a regular pub crawl as his depression firmly took hold.

While his noose made a brief appearance in 1824 following the execution of Joseph Dale for the murder of William Wood, he was growing ever more dependent on his income as a rat-catcher and he loathed every moment of it. While rat catching was a means to an end, he was beginning to feel that his role was becoming diminished as the city's executioner. Furthermore, he began to feel the mockery of the local press and his fellow Cestrians. The once infamous, arrogant stride around the streets of Chester that had previously installed fear among those who saw it had diminished severely.

Yet, Burrows was fully aware of the law and was more than happy to submit anyone who was brave enough to stand against him to the power of the courts. In order to remind people about who he was, Burrows continued to roam the streets with his noose in hand as his drinking gathered pace.

One such incident that caught the attention of newspaper editors was that of an altercation with Thomas Roby in September 1825, after which Burrows was brought to the courts on a charge of assault. Burrows would often stroll along the Shambles on Northgate Street, keen to remember his former career as a butcher and chat to those who knew him well. Burrows' allegation was that Roby, unprovoked, kicked him down on the street and then violently kicked him on the shins. In his view of events, he was just harmlessly minding his own business before being attacked.[3]

However, Roby's evidence was quite different. Standing before the court, Roby testified his innocence, stating that: 'Upon my word and honour it's all a lie, and if you'll believe him then you'll believe anything … He was staring drunk and when I went towards him, he fell down. I'll bring all the women in the Shambles to prove his misconduct.'[4]

Burrows had been drunk and this was becoming a regular sight around the streets of Chester. Walking around with his noose in hand, he was alleged to have been 'swaggering … and telling how you hung folks'.[5] Burrows' arrogance and desire to be noticed had caught up with him.

Incensed by Burrows' behaviour, Roby gave the hangman a nudge that knocked Burrows off balance in his already inebriated state, upon which he fell on to the street. While Burrows claimed that this was a lie, Roby called for a witness to corroborate his side of events. Mrs Smathers stated that Roby only 'pushed Burrows'.

With his pride dented, Burrows had been determined to take this small incident to court but if he believed that it garnered him any respect then he was sorely mistaken. The *Chester Chronicle* was more than happy to mock the hangman in an article full of puns relating to his profession. In its summing up of the case, the *Chronicle* reported that: 'Burrows was asked if he was inclined to *Drop* the matter if Roby would promise not to attack him in future?'[6] The case was eventually thrown out, much to Burrows' dismay. Yet the case did provide Burrows with an element of protection, discouraging others from attacking him just because of this profession.

It was not the only incident where he would receive ridicule at the hands of the local press. On Good Friday in 1826, Burrows found himself in trouble once again, only on this occasion there was no one to blame but himself.

The *Chester Chronicle* claimed that Burrows had received a retainer from a neighbouring town for his services and would go on to spend his unexpected windfall while being 'rather elevated in spirits'.[7] The editor highlighted the use of the word 'spirits' by underlining the word, showing that Burrows' reputation for drink was common knowledge throughout Chester.

The article continued by saying that: 'Sammy gulped his spirituous libations so that, by three o'clock the finisher of the law was himself – finished – and that he who had taken in so much was at last kicked out and being unable to gain equilibrium, he was wallowing in the gutter "drunk as a sow".'[8]

Once again, drink became Burrows' undoing as he was charged with being drunk on Good Friday. Receiving a retaining fee from another principality for his noose, Burrows quickly spent it in Northgate Street. Moving from pub to pub he was later found in the gutter as a group of youths managed to tie a rope around his neck and lifted him into a hand barrow before parading him around the area in his drunken state.

When Burrows appeared at the house of corrections he certainly did not have the appearance of a dishevelled drunk. Instead he 'looked as demure and sleek as a puritan'. The embarrassment to the local authorities made them take the case seriously enough to fine him 5 shillings and costs, and yet despite this he retained his position as the city's executioner.[9]

Burrows' drinking was getting out of hand and was a continued source of concern to those in charge of his employment. Regularly prior to executions, people were sent out to look for Burrows in order to see if he was drunk. If he was, then he was taken to gaol in order to prevent him from getting even worse and to sober up before he could complete his task.

The changes taking place around Burrows were too much for him to accept without alcohol. He was dealing with the grief of losing Henry, seeing his youngest son transported, and of course the fact that his once-feared profession was in constant danger of being eradicated altogether. With so many convicts slipping through his grasp, he began to feel as if he was becoming redundant, and with his ever-increasing consumption of alcohol, he was no longer feared but pitied.

Chapter 17

Tears of the Hangman

The Execution of Joseph Woodhouse and John Henshall
New City Gaol, Chester, 1829

REVEREND WILLIAM CLARKE listened intently to every word that the dying hangman uttered on his deathbed in Brook Street. Yet, he felt that his message of the need to ask the Lord for forgiveness was not entirely getting through. Burrows, in Clarke's mind, seemed somewhat proud of what he did as he spoke about those who he sent to eternity rather than showing any genuine signs of remorse. Surely there must have been at least one execution where the brutish Burrows felt some kind of guilt?

Clarke asked Burrows if any execution made him feel uneasy. Samuel stared at him briefly before looking away from the reverend's gaze and focusing on his hands. He remained silent. Clarke knew there was at least one of the condemned men's plights that had revealed Burrows was human rather than the showboating brute that nearly everyone in Chester knew. Then, after a moment, Burrows began to sob uncontrollably.

As he lifted his head, tears streamed from Burrows' eyes. Clarke fetched him some water and handed it to the shaking Samuel, who swiftly rejected it. He needed something stronger to recant this particular memory that he thought he had hidden away in the back of his mind.

Clarke remembered the occasion all too well. As he had stood next to Burrows on that particular day he saw a very different side to the hangman. As chaplain of the New City Gaol and the house of correction, Clarke held a number of responsibilities. He would give a service to all prisoners within its confines every Wednesday, Friday, and twice on the Sabbath day. With most prisoners, his aim was to help them to find God ahead of their eventual release. Yet, for some, their release would be into the hands of the Lord as he gave the final sacrament to the condemned.

Witnessing a strong man like Burrows in tears always made Clarke feel uncomfortable but with time running out for the hangman, the reverend felt the need to end the silence quickly. He did so by asking Burrows if he remembered the name of the young man that they were talking about.

Burrows looked up with watery red eyes as Clarke placed his hand on his shoulder in order to comfort him. Burrows nodded and simply replied, 'Henshall, John Henshall.'

Burrows began the day of 26 September 1829 much in the same way that he did before any execution. He knew that a double execution awaited him and there was one of the two men who he was particularly looking forward to dispatching. Sitting alongside Mary, the couple ate their breakfast, with the conversation primarily being about the awful crimes of Joseph Woodhouse. It was a crime that particularly disgusted Mary. As he departed he turned to Mary, who waved him off and said that she would be there for this one.

Mary was not alone in intending to be there for the execution as the largest crowd ever to assemble in front of the New City Gaol gathered to witness the spectacle. As Samuel Burrows ventured into town from Brook Street even he could sense something a bit different about this particular event. On one hand, there was a level of excitement regarding the execution of Woodhouse, a man who was universally loathed for his crime. On the other hand, there was also a sense of sorrow with regard to the other man who faced Burrows' noose.

Burrows, as always, gave John Henshall no particular thought as he walked down Watergate Street towards the gaol. All he could think about was Woodhouse. There were certain crimes that boiled even the hardened hangman's blood and as far as he was concerned the crime of child rape was among the worst. The evidence against Woodhouse came from his own family following the brutal rape of his 11-year-old daughter.[1] Much to the public galleries' amazement at the Summer Assizes, it was later revealed that this was not the first instance of his heinous crimes against his daughter. In summing up, the Assize judge revealed that this was the third time that Woodhouse had been found guilty of the offence, and with an inability to change his behaviour the sentence of death was pronounced.[2]

The testimony of Woodhouse's two other children proved to be pivotal alongside that of his sister-in-law in condemning him to death.[3] As news spread of his crime, the hatred towards him from the Cestrian masses intensified. Fearing repercussions from the crowd, the authorities opted to transfer him from Chester Castle to the New City Gaol in the earliest hours of the morning so that he could arrive unharmed before his eventual drop.

As Burrows arrived he had already gathered what he needed for his work and quickly made his nooses before inspecting the gallows and testing the mechanism of the bolt that would release the trapdoor. With no crowds around him, the sound of the release reverberated around the Linenhall, scaring the nearby birds to fly away. Resetting the long drop, Burrows felt more than prepared for what was to come. He stood high above Chester as the day was beginning for many. The sound of wooden carts clattering along the cobbled road echoed around him as he saw those about to begin their days. From his vantage point he felt even more unique than usual.

He had never been this prepared before and following the executions of John Leir and John Proudlove in the spring he felt that he had to get this one right. On that particular occasion, Burrows was found the night previous in a drunken stake. Knowing that he was due to perform his duties the next day, the authorities of Chester were keeping a close eye on him before eventually deciding to bring him into New City Gaol, where a cell was waiting for him to sleep it off. Being forcibly escorted and dragged through the streets of Chester was never a good look but he could not deny that spending the night in the cells had made it possible for him to do his job the next day.

Burrows took a deep breath as he looked around his stage, imagining the rapturous cheers that he would soon receive as Woodhouse dropped. He had not paid much attention to the other man who would join Woodhouse on the gallows but it would soon become a moment that Burrows would never forget as it lingered with him until his dying breath.

John Henshall simply wanted to be liked. It was not much to ask for but he was about to join with friends who were more sinister than him. The 20-year-old from Dunham Massey was the son of a hard-working farmer who had befriended the wrong sort and formed a small poaching gang.

The gang opted to poach on the land of the Earl of Stamford. Tired of the ongoing situation, and with little protection from the authorities, the earl had assembled a group of gamekeepers to protect his land from further incidents. Whether Henshall or the gang that he had joined knew this is unknown.

Henshall and the rest of the gang were caught and cornered as they entered the Earl's estate. Soon, threats of violence were shouted across the field and gunfire sounded. One of the Earl's gamekeepers was shot and wounded. As the gang went their separate ways, Henshall was caught, arrested, and then moved to Chester Castle to await the Summer Assizes.[4]

Rural crimes such as poaching were on the rise in the 1820s and it was a trend that the establishment were keen to stamp out. Henshall was about to become the county's deterrent. Other members of the gang were subsequently caught and, fearing for their own lives, they claimed that it was Henshall who fired the shot that wounded the gamekeeper. Turning King's evidence, they went unpunished as Henshall faced the ultimate reprisal. It was an event that caused Mr Justice Jervis, a man who had previously written to the Home Secretary Robert Peel regarding opposition to his reforms, to weep as he passed sentence. Despite having to condemn Henshall to the gallows, Justice Jervis was visibly moved by what had happened.[5]

The public sympathy for Henshall was great, although Samuel Burrows had not thought about it too much. Arrogantly, he still firmly believed in the law and held to the belief that he was a man of that law. Yet, when he met Henshall, albeit briefly, his attitude would change.

While Burrows had a natural hatred towards Woodhouse and pinioned him with a certain sense of glee, his feelings quickly switched as he entered the ante-room where Henshall awaited his date with the hangman. Visibly shaking and clinging on to the words of Reverend Hoskins, who was aiming to comfort him with religious verse, Henshall was uncontrollably weeping as the last moments of his life were approaching. As the reverend urged him to say the Lord's Prayer with him, Henshall attempted to do so loudly as much as his shaking voice would allow him.

Burrows watched and turned to Reverend Clarke and Sheriff Thomas Bowers, whose tears were slowly trickling down their cheeks. Samuel asked Bowers what the young man had done to find himself here. Bowers, holding back the tears, further told Burrows about Henshall's case and the unfairness of the whole situation. Sheriff George Allender was said to have become so overcome by emotion 'that he was compelled to retire into the next room'.[6]

Burrows, a man so hardened by his experiences as the city's executioner, thought about the situation that he had found himself in. He saw Reverend Hoskins and Clarke trying to remain strong for the sake of Henshall before turning back to Bowers, who was now weeping. Burrows was about to hang a young man who was around the same age as his boy Charles. Thoughts of Charles in Van Diemen's Land rushed through his mind as he stared at Henshall. Given his crime, why was he not heading to Van Diemen's Land himself? The realisation hit Burrows hard: this could have been Charles sitting before him.

Despite trying to remain as hard-faced as he possibly could, Burrows inevitably broke down in the same way as Sheriff Bowers, who was standing beside him. It was a rare moment in Burrows' life where he had actually let his guard down in front of others.[7] Drink was his method of dealing with his grief for both Henry and now, Charles. He had carried on as was expected using any vice he could in order to ease his pain. Now, it had all come out. The unfairness of it all overwhelmed him as Henshall surrendered himself to him and allowed the hangman to pin him with a rope around his arms.

Burrows left the ante-room and joined Sheriff Allender. The pair sat in silence as they contemplated what still needed to be done. The law of the land must be fulfilled, even if it felt wrong to do so. Allender was surprised to see Burrows like this. Usually, he was brazen in his duties to the point where Allender felt that it was distasteful. Yet in this moment, Burrows gave him a fleeting piece of his humanity. Nothing needed to be said between the two men as they dried their tears before escorting Woodhouse and Henshall in front of the Cestrian crowd.

As the two men ascended the scaffold, the crowd beneath them displayed a mixture of disgust at Woodhouse and sympathy for Henshall. Burrows felt uneasy as he adjusted the noose around Henshall's neck and placed a handkerchief between his fingers. Uncharacteristically, Burrows placed his hand on Henshall's shoulders. He did not need to say anything but it was Burrows' way of saying sorry for what was about to come.

The two men stood there for nearly four minutes as Henshall begged that the Lord should receive his soul. The crowd beneath remained silent in prayer for his soul before beginning to sob aloud for the young man. Burrows' eyes were firmly fixated on Henshall's handkerchief but the longer it went on he began to cry once again. Mary, standing in the crowd, was watching him as his shoulders slowly began to shake. All she wanted to do was to comfort him as she began to weep. Then Henshall dropped the handkerchief. Burrows waited until it hit the wooden floor, and then released the bolt.[8]

Shrieks of horror emanated from the crowd as the two men dropped. Both died almost instantly.

Henshall's father waited for Burrows to cut his son down. He had arranged for a cart to return his son home. The two men gazed at each other. Both fathers experienced their grief in different ways. Mr Henshall did not blame Burrows for what he did as both men lovingly placed John Henshall into his coffin before putting him on to the cart.

Taking the young man's body home, the family allowed members of the village to pay their respects to Henshall, raising money from those who wished to see him before he was buried underneath his grandfather's coffin in an attempt to ensure he would be undisturbed in eternal peace.[9]

Laying in his bed in his Brook Street room, Burrows was a shadow of the man who had hanged John Henshall that day. Weak and infirm, the once-hardened hangman was only days away from death. There was still more to say to Reverend Clarke but he had one burning question that he felt compelled to ask.

Burrows asked Reverend Clarke if God could ever forgive him for what he did to Henshall? The reverend stated that the Lord could only ever forgive those who truly repented their sins and sincerely meant it. Burrows glanced up at Clarke as the tears continued to steam from his eyes. His lips trembled as he asked Clarke if this was the face of a sincere man.

Clarke nodded, the tears of the hangman were enough for the Lord to see his sincerity. Burrows was not in the mood to talk anymore, instead, he turned over and looked at the wall away from Clarke. The reverend knew that their session was over for the day. He promised to return the next morning before recanting the Lord's Prayer to Burrows before he left.

Chapter 18

When the Hangman Came to Beaumaris

The Execution of William Griffith
Beaumaris, Anglesey, 1830

THE BARREN YEARS that Samuel Burrows had faced since the repeal of the Waltham Black Act had seen him turn into everything he despised more than anything. The once frequent executions at what was now dubbed 'Sammy's Castle' had become memories. The fear that he had once instilled in his fellow Cestrians was now slowly ebbing away as he found himself in a damaging financial situation.

While Burrows still received a retainer for his services from the city, it was simply not enough to keep him going after such a long time without an execution. Burrows had not pulled the lever for some time and as time went on he began to wonder if he would ever pull it again.

Desperately seeking an alternative, the sheer level of his unpopularity soon dawned on him. Believing that his skills as a butcher could one day save him in case of this eventuality, he was dealt a swift lesson in rejection. The notorious hangman on hard times was someone nobody wanted to employ, especially one who had been as brazen in the enjoyment of his work as Burrows.

In order to supplement his dwindling income, Burrows had no option but to find work in one of the lowest occupations around. From the heights of his castle, he had fallen back to earth in a massive way to become a freelance rat-catcher where the city would pay him for every rat that he caught. Thankfully for Burrows, rats were a plentiful resource in Chester and he would use some of his retainer to purchase the necessary traps, which he would place around areas where he knew they would thrive. While the job allowed him to keep his head above water, it was far from the life to which he had grown accustomed.

Thankfully for Burrows, his notoriety had expanded further afield than Chester as he offered his services to anyone who was looking for his experience. It wouldn't take long for the offers to come in.

When the offer of work came to him he simply could not believe his luck. Beaumaris was preparing for the execution of William Griffith but the authorities faced a major issue. No one in the area was prepared to do it. Due to Griffith being executed for the attempted murder of his wife Mary, the townsfolk had turned against the idea of the ultimate punishment, largely due to the fact that the woman was still alive. While an executioner was hard enough to find, the authorities of Beaumaris also had other problems. Men in the area had refused to erect the scaffold and a feared uprising meant that more constables would need to be employed to control the crowd on the day of execution in case of a riot.[1]

In order to compensate for all of these issues, the authorities of Beaumaris were prepared to spend more than any other township in order to get the job done. Carpenters were brought in from as far as Liverpool at a cost of £1,013 in order to build the scaffold and a bridge from the inside of the gaol to the outer wall. With that particular deal done, all Beaumaris needed was an executioner.

The offer on the table was the highest Burrows had ever seen and one that the City of Chester was all too eager to accept. The city would receive £6 and 6 shillings in order to obtain the services of Burrows. A retainer of £3 was paid directly to him. On top of this, a further £7 was paid to transport Burrows from Chester to Beaumaris, some 70 miles away, including any expenses required on his journey. Once Griffith was hanged, Burrows would be paid a further £17. The offer was an exceptionally generous one. For only a few days away and a single morning's work, Burrows would earn the equivalent of more than three months' pay as a skilled worker in any other field. It did not take him long to agree to the deal.[2]

Burrows had a spring in his step as he made his way to his trusted ropemaker. Thomas Whittle had been supplying rope to the hangman ever since the two men found each other following Burrows' first bungled execution. While Burrows was more than happy to have anyone supply him with rope, Whittle was not only the closest to the New City Gaol but also nearest to Northgate Street. The proximity of Whittle's shop on King Street meant that Burrows could also easily sneak in a quick drink before getting his hands on the rope he needed prior to any execution. Despite the likes of Thomas Harrison being closer to his new home in Brook Street, Burrows felt that going anywhere else would be bad form. Burrows trusted Whittle and he had never let him down. Entering Whittle's shop, Thomas welcomed Burrows with open arms but was confused given how he had not heard of any forthcoming executions in Chester. It allowed Burrows to tell Whittle more about his trip to Anglesey and the offer that was too good to refuse.[3]

With his retainer from Beaumaris and new ropes supplied by Whittle in hand, Burrows did what anyone with a fondness for alcohol did. He went to the public house and quickly spent most of his retainer, telling anyone who would listen about his latest deal and his upcoming trip to Anglesey. As the drink flowed, so too did his story about the grizzly crime that Griffith had committed and the bizarre situation in Beaumaris that had led to his new lucrative position. While Burrows did not know it at the time, this particular execution would be one of his most difficult to date. Either way, Burrows felt that he was important once again and if the people of Chester loathed him, then he simply did not care. His gloating and new-found riches meant that Sammy was back to his old self and he made sure that the whole city knew it as he stumbled from each public house on Northgate Street.

Anglesey had never needed a permanent executioner. The rural island just off the north-western tip of Wales had only ever previously executed five individuals on its own gallows. The last execution had been in 1786, when John Ellis was hanged for stealing from a dwelling house[4] and since then, the isle had not known the commotion of such an event. Now, forty-four years later, Samuel Burrows was about to come to town for a one-off show. It had been a long wait for the people of Anglesey and tensions were already running high with the thought of the hanging at the outer wall of the newly built Beaumaris Gaol.

Beaumaris Gaol had been officially open for less than a year at the time it was preparing for its first public execution. The new gaol was built partly with the spectacle of public execution in mind. The gaol itself was encased within a high wall. Its imposing perimeter was similar to others but Beaumaris had an extra macabre feature. On the gaol wall alongside Steeple Lane, the gallows door acted as a constant reminder to the inhabitants of Beaumaris about the consequences of any crimes. The door, adjacent to the first floor of the gaol, was designed to ensure that the scaffold could be firmly built around it. The bell above the door would ring in order to allow the crowd to converge and for the condemned to witness their final moments in front of them.[5]

The cell for the condemned would not be far away and situated on the first floor of the gaol. It would be here where the prisoner would await their eventual execution. As mentioned, a small temporary bridge was built between the gaol and its surrounding wall in order to allow access to the gallows door. There would be no doubt that the prisoner would have heard its construction as their day of reckoning approached. It would have only been a short walk for them to reach their final destination.

Despite the execution door being such a key focal point of the outer wall of the gaol, it would only be used twice during the period of public executions. William Griffith would be the first man to face the ultimate punishment at the newly built gaol.

He and Mary had separated briefly before William tried to kill her. On 2 April 1830, he went to the couple's home hoping to talk about their relationship. Inside the house in Newborough, Anglesey, was Mary and the couple's daughter. When Griffith arrived Mary would have been on guard given her husband's temperament, but whether or not he forced himself on her, we simply do not know.

Once inside, the conversation began to anger Griffith and he became violent. The couple's daughter, seeing her father begin to beat her mother, fled the house to call on neighbours to help. When she returned to her home with someone, the full scene of the attack shocked them.

Mary was found with her head beneath the fire grate of the fireplace. She was covered in hot coals that had burnt her face and body. Marks around her neck led them to believe that she had also been strangled. A stick had also used to beat her and then forced down her throat. Despite the gruesome scene that Griffith's daughter was now witnessing, her father was nowhere to be seen. Amazingly, despite the ordeal that she had faced, Mary was still alive.

It would not take long for the jury to find Griffith guilty of attempted murder. Given the ferocious nature of the attack, Judge Raine had no option but to impose the maximum sentence. But the judge allowed Griffith more time between sentencing and his eventual execution as he believed that more work was needed to be done to deliver this soul into the arms of Christ before he departed this world.

It would prove to be a challenge to get Griffith to display any form of remorse for what he had done. Despite many attempts from the local religious orders, Griffith rejected the word of God. To those who attempted to guide him towards the gates of forgiveness, they would later state that he 'died as he had lived, without any manifestation of Christian feeling or even of manly firmness'.[6]

He would not even show any remorse towards his own wife following the attack. The day after his sentencing, he was allowed to see her. Once again, Griffith remained cold. If anything, according to the *North Wales Chronicle*, he believed that it was unfair that he should die and that she should live.

The Noose of Samuel Burrows

If Samuel Burrows thought that this would be an easy execution then Griffith had other plans. He had already tried to escape his fate but was then caught trying to break free from his cell.

It was a long journey by coach. Thankfully for Burrows, the additional £7 that the authorities allowed for his journey was already partly spent and he was feeling slightly light-headed by the time that he approached the Menai Bridge. Opened four years previously, Burrows looked on in awe as the carriage approached. Designed by Thomas Telford, the suspension bridge was one of the first of its kind. Previously, the journey would have taken even more time as the strait between the mainland and the isle had to be navigated by ferry. The unpredictability of the strong tidal flows on the strait also made the journey more precarious. Ferries could often capsize, resulting in the loss of essential goods needed by those who lived in Anglesey, although there had been other dire consequences. In 1785, a boat carrying fifty-five people found itself in trouble and ran aground on a sandbank. In fear of the strait's natural currents and whirlpools, the crew attempted to free the vessel. The boat began to fill with water as rescuers from Carnarvon were summoned. As the conditions deteriorated further, the rescue boat could not reach the scene in time. Only one person survived.[7]

For Burrows, there would be no repeat of the incident of 1785 as his carriage proceeded over Telford's new megastructure. As the executioner was arriving in town with relative ease and luxury, the same could not be said for William Griffith, who was waiting in the condemned cell prior to his execution and pondering his final moments.

The scaffolders from Liverpool had completed their job by the time Burrows arrived at the gaol. With little to do after his long journey, the hangman was ready to retire to his room. Burrows was greeted at the gates and escorted to the governor's bedroom on the first floor of the gaol, where he would board for the night. The room was ideal and more than spacious for one person. A luxurious bed and a roaring fire awaited him as he wandered around the room and made himself at home. Soon his meal and a bottle of ale would arrive before he could rest.

Just opposite where Burrows was boarding for the night in relative luxury, Griffith was pondering his final night on Earth. The condemned cell at Beaumaris was twice the size of the normal cells within the gaol and was the only one that had its own fireplace. It would be the only item that the two men would have in common as the executioner, only metres away, drifted off to sleep. While Burrows slept soundly, Griffith was wide awake and becoming melancholic about his own impending fate.

Griffith was becoming more unstable, bursting into states of melancholy and despair. But on the morning of 15 September 1830, he was more than prepared to fight anyone who approached him, even Burrows.

That morning Griffith had already laid siege to his own cell. In a fit of rage he had destroyed it and used his wooden bed to jar his cell door closed so no one could enter. The guards had no choice but to break the door down and force Griffith into submission. Soon the firm footsteps of Burrows would fill the corridor. With every step, Griffith knew that the hangman was finally coming for him.[8]

Burrows was no slouch when it came to this kind of situation. While he would have preferred for the condemned to have made their peace with God prior to execution, he was more than prepared to force the issue. In a situation like this, Burrows would have to wrestle against the criminal and force him to the ground. Once there, Burrows would then restrain his prey further with a rope around the wrists and legs. Whether Griffith liked it or not, he would be executed and Burrows would get his payday.

Leaving the cell, Griffith was dragged down the corridor by the gaolers as Burrows walked ahead of them. Each step filled the corridor, echoing around the gaol as the bell on top of the gallows door began to toll. Burrows did not need to look behind him as he strode confidently towards the door. With each booming stride of the hangman, Griffith continued to struggle with every inch of his life against the gaolers, who were fighting to contain him. As the door of the gaol opened, the bright

The Noose of Samuel Burrows

sun shone through, forcing Burrows to squint as they adjusted to the sunlight. The crowd, although still out of sight, could clearly be heard as the decibels rose. These people, although heavily policed, were still making their ill feelings about the execution perfectly clear. Walking over the makeshift bridge, the gallows door opened as Burrows took in his first glimpse of his latest audience.

He was warned the previous night about an apparent plot to free Griffith from his gallows and he could see the extra constables that were promised as they scuffled with members of the crowd to hold them back. This was no time for his usual showboating that often entertained the Chester crowds as the events of the morning had already been unlike any other execution he was used to. The fight with Griffith had already taken it out of Burrows and he was beginning to sense that this execution was far from over. With his senses heightened, he looked around to see Griffith continue to struggle.

Despite being tightly fastened by his wrists and ankles, Griffith continued to fight against his inevitable fate. Using only his head, he fought against Burrows, headbutting the hangman as he tried to place a black hood over his head. Each successful evasion from the hangman's hood was greeted with a chorus of cheers as the crowd willed Griffith on in his battle against Burrows. The gaolers grabbed Griffith once again as they aimed to contain him and silence the crowd. Burrows was far from impressed. No one had ever fought him in the way Griffith had so far. What he thought was going to be a routine, straightforward payday, was becoming a nightmare as the crowd continued to cheer for the condemned man.[9]

With the hood now on, Griffith continued his struggle as Burrows reached for his noose. He urged the gaolers to hold him still so he could place the noose around his neck but Griffith continued to fight. Eventually, Burrows managed to get the noose around Griffith's neck, walked towards the lever and pulled.

Griffith plummeted 15ft as the crowd took a sharp intake of breath. All they could see was that Griffith was no longer on the platform as black cloth surrounded the place of the final drop. The silence that filled the air was only broken with the sound of taut rope as Burrows left the stage abruptly. Griffith would hang for an hour as the crowd slowly dispersed.

There was still work to do for Burrows as he still had to cut his condemned man down but for now he retired to the governor's bedroom to take stock of what had just happened. As he washed his face, he noticed some blood in the bowl. He touched his lip to check if that was where the blood was coming from. Griffith's headbutt had caught him square in the jaw but Burrows felt nothing. The adrenaline eased the pain at the time but now, as he started to relax, he finally felt it.

With Steeple Lane now empty, Burrows still approached the final phase of his work with caution. Anyone could be waiting to pounce on him through a desire to claim Griffith's lifeless body. Despite being found guilty of attempted murder, the court had ordered that his body should be buried within the walls of the gaol rather than being released to family members. Cutting down the body, Burrows remained on high alert until he had safely returned the corpse to the boundaries of the gaol. With a long journey ahead of him, Burrows opted to stay one more night before returning to Chester first thing in the morning.

The execution of Griffith had taken its toll and for the first time in a long while Burrows began to feel his 58 years of age. Griffith would never leave Beaumaris Gaol, even in death. He was buried in a lime pit near the wall of the gaol in order to dissolve his body. In order to add further punishment, he was buried standing up to ensure that he would never gain eternal rest.[10]

For Burrows, the morning could not come soon enough. While he was thankful to receive his money, he was also relieved to jump back on the coach to return home. It had been a gruelling job and Burrows' mind began to wonder as to how much longer he could do it. Whether it be the unpredictability of when he would work again or the physicality of the job, his future as a hangman was in doubt but at least he had a long journey to contemplate it.

Chapter 19

The Hat on the Wye

The Executions of Joseph Pugh, John Matthews and William Williams
Hereford Gaol, 1832

SAMUEL BURROWS WAS beginning to think that the city of Chester had forgotten that they even had a hangman. Since the double execution of Joseph Woodhouse and Joseph Henshall, he had found himself slowly losing any true meaning within the city. It had been the second-longest barren period of his career and almost three years since he last performed in front of the Cestrian crowd.

But that was not to say that he had not been busy with his noose. Even though the Chester masses may not have seen him command the local crowd in the ways that they were accustomed to for so long, Burrows was far from quiet. Instead, it was other parts of the country that were now witnessing him at work.

Following a successful yet draining experience in Beaumaris, Burrows was still a much-needed man, even though the populace of his home city may have thought that he was considering calling time on his exploits. Now his services were required elsewhere yet again and he was informed of a trip to Hereford, where he had worked before.

When told about the triple execution of Joseph Pugh, John Matthews, and William Williams, his heart sank and he released a heavy sigh.

Burrows should have been happy about the news; after all, a triple execution was a highly lucrative trip for any hangman, but at the age of 61 years old, he was beginning to feel the strain more so than he had previously. The hangman was growing tired of the physicality of his work, especially following his trip to Beaumaris. Yet, his choices were quickly evaporating around him. Mary was becoming more frail and Samuel was convinced that she was feeling worse than what she told him. The income from the triple execution would allow him to take more care of her but Burrows' ever-growing dependence on alcohol usually meant that whatever his best intentions were, the money would be spent at Chester's many local inns.

With little option, he accepted the job and slowly headed back to his Brook Street home in order to pack a small bag before returning to the Exchange to board his coach. Mary was becoming used to her husband leaving the city for days on end and, despite reassuring him that she was in good health, Samuel remained sceptical. He handed her some of the money that he had received for his travel expenses and urged her to see a doctor before picking up his bag and slowly closing the door behind him.

The prospect of another long journey filled Burrows with a sense of dread. It was an experience that he used to relish in his younger days but as his years advanced he felt that it was now becoming too much of a burden for him. His income from rat-catching was enough to ensure that the Burrows of Brook Street did not starve and his retainer as the county executioner barely gave them much more. With Mary now in ill health, Burrows knew that he had to accept anything that came his way. He grew angry with himself and the situation that he had found himself in as he walked through the streets of Chester. As he muttered to himself, he felt the need for a drink more than ever. It did not last long as one was swiftly downed before the coach arrived.

Susan Connop needed a property and she needed one quickly. She knew that soon the town of Hereford would be a hotbed of activity as the Lent Assizes paid their annual visit. As always, Connop knew an opportunity to make some easy money and was equipped with the assets to make even more. Soon the town would be full of judges, barristers, and other well-to-do members of society who were looking to let off some steam. Sensing her chance, she made the journey from Worcester to make some hay as the sun shone. Once arriving in Hereford, she already knew exactly where she needed to go.

Joseph Pugh was expecting her. The pair had previously worked together, albeit briefly, when she last visited Hereford. Arriving with some of her best girls, she greeted Pugh and asked him if they should set up in the usual way. Pugh was all too eager to please, knowing the riches that were also coming his way. For allowing Connop and her girls to stay with him he knew that he would receive a percentage of whatever the girls made over the coming days. For the next few days, Susan Connop was bringing her little Worcester brothel to Pugh's house in Quaker's Lane.[1]

The girls quickly went to work. Some would stay in the house welcoming those who had already heard about their upcoming visit to the town. Others would leave the house in order to encourage men to stop by for a visit. Setting up shop, the girls knew that once the Lent Assizes were in full swing then so too would be their little illicit pop-up business. It would not take long before Walter Carwardine would visit them.

Carwardine was 60 years old, overweight, and a heavy drinker. The farmer from Kinnersley was in town for more legitimate business at the Lent Assizes in the form of a lawsuit against one of his brothers. It was a messy family affair that Walter took no pleasure from but with his appearance at the Assizes completed, he felt the need for some much-needed hospitality. He ventured to the Horse and Groom public house in Eign Street, where he stayed for some time before moving on to the Red Streak.

It was around here where he was picked up by one of Susan Connop's girls. Carwardine had taken a shine to Susan Reignart, who took him back to Pugh's home on Quaker's Lane. Once there, Reignart did her best to encourage him to stay. He made himself comfortable on Pugh's armchair where he was plied with ever-increasing amounts of gin as Reignart sat on his knee.

Sarah Coley, another of Connop's girls, decided that it was her turn to entertain Carwardine as Reignart took another man to the bedroom. Flirting with him, she encouraged more gin as the idea of actually sleeping with him repulsed her. Thankfully, Carwardine was practically completely intoxicated. With money in his pocket and now completely inebriated, Carwardine was ripe for the taking. Coley showed Connop some of the money that she stole from him and was encouraged to put it in her pocket.[2] It would not take long before the farmer was encouraged to find where to lay his head for a night away from Quaker's Lane. Sarah Coley offered to help him to find somewhere given the drunken state that he was in and, agreeing reluctantly, Carwardine left the bawdy house with her.[3]

Susan Connop was beginning to feel a bit edgy about the whole situation but her primary concern was not for Walter Carwardine but for Sarah Coley. Concerned for her well-being, Connop ventured out into the streets to find her. A few minutes later, she returned with Coley. Suddenly, William Williams and John Matthews burst through the door, slamming it behind them. Then there was a loud knocking. It was Walter Carwardine. The street was silent no more as his booming voice reverberated down the lane.

'Open the door, for I am robbed!' Carwardine cried as he continued to bang on the door.

Williams was sent to the door in an attempt to calm the situation. Connop told Williams to make the drunk declare throughout the street that he was not robbed in the house as it would be bad for business. Williams was followed by Pugh, who was now feeling agitated by the stand-off. He was heard saying: 'Damn your eyes, if you don't be off, I'll send you.'[4]

Williams, Matthews, and Pugh spoke to Carwardine outside. Susan Reignart was alone in bed when she was startled out of her slumber an hour later. She was awoken by a commotion taking place downstairs. She heard and felt a crash so loud that even the staircase shook with the force.[5]

The long journey to Hereford had all but wiped out Samuel Burrows. Arriving at the gaol, he was more than ready to rest his weary head before fulfilling his duties the next day. Getting out of his carriage, he could clearly see the recently erected gallows above the gatehouse entrance of the building. Knowing that he would be spending the night within the confines of the gaol, he opted to be sent to his room so he could prepare the three nooses that he would be using.

It was unusual for Burrows to be behaving so professionally. Perhaps he had mellowed with age, he thought to himself. Maybe the lust for his profession that he had previously shown was slowly ebbing away, but then again, it could have been the tiredness after such a long journey. Either way, Burrows simply wanted to get the job done so he could return home.

He was recognised by those who had worked with him during his last trip to Hereford. Pleasantries were exchanged but in reality it was merely small talk as Burrows longed for something to eat and drink before heading to sleep. He was asked if he remembered much about the last man who he executed here. Of course, Burrows remembered. He might not have remembered the name but the young man's limp was certainly something you did not forget.

The man Burrows executed that day was convicted of the highway robbery of Francis Wellington, an elderly former soldier who was walking home when he was attacked and robbed of his pension money. It would ultimately mean that James Williams would stand on the gallows as Burrows placed a noose around his neck before pulling the lever and sending him to meet his maker.[6] Little did Burrows care at the time that James Williams' brother was among the crowd that saw Burrows complete his awful duty. Now, William Williams was awaiting the same fate as his younger brother and would immediately recognise Burrows as the man who sent James into eternity.

Following the altercation at Quaker's Lane, Walter Carwardine simply vanished. He never made it back to his farm in Kinnersley but the question on everybody's lips was, where was he?

Days later, Thomas Pearce found Carwardine's hat floating on the wharf at Monk's Hole on the River Wye. Sensing that this was valuable information, Pearce approached Walter's brother, William.

The Hat on the Wye

William Carwardine was already actively searching for his lost brother. Despite the family situation that had led to Walter's appearance at the Lent Assizes, William had no ill will towards him. William scoured the area where Walter was last seen but news that his brother's hat had been discovered on the river began to fill him with dread. Pearce and Carwardine agreed to search the river once more alongside bargeman James Price. It would be Price who would eventually find the floating and entangled corpse of Walter Carwardine.[7]

Even upon the discovery, William thought that perhaps Walter had simply stumbled and fell into the river while drunk. After all, why would anyone actually want to kill him? Walter's body, however, revealed exactly what happened to him. The post-mortem indicated that he had several wounds around his head. Although it could not be said exactly which injury was the fatal blow, it was concluded that he did not drown. It was believed that he was attacked, murdered, and then disposed of in the River Wye. It was deemed that the cause of death was that of strangulation and that more than one assailant must have been involved.

Suspicions and gossip swiftly swirled around Walter Carwardine's final night and particular attention was drawn towards the bawdy house kept by Joseph Pugh. It did not take the authorities long to call him in. Here he revealed that Susan Connop had used the house that particular night. She too was brought in and the next time the Assizes returned to Hereford, she found herself in the dock rather than servicing her clientele.

The subsequent trial was eventually halted by Justice Patterson midway through as he deemed that there was insufficient evidence to proceed, even though the circumstances surrounding Carwardine's eventual fate were suspicious. Both Pugh and Connop walked free... for now.[8]

Burrows knew nothing about the first trial and the name of Susan Connop was nowhere to be seen on his small list of those due to be executed in front of Hereford Gaol. From his previous experience in Hereford,

Burrows knew the drill already. Pinion the men, then head up to the top of the gatehouse, where he knew the crowd would be salivating to see the men drop. With Hereford using a similar gallows to the one he had in Chester, he knew that this would be a straightforward job.

He would not even need to take their bodies to the infirmary for dissection after he had cut them down as he was advised that men would arrive in order to do that for him. It was easy money for the Chester hangman, yet he was growing unfulfilled by his duties. Burrows was beginning to loathe these kinds of trips, mainly because he was instructed not to showboat and had to deal with the situation with respect. In Chester, he felt like an arm of the law; a man to be wary of and an entertainer to boot. In Hereford, he felt like an outsider simply brought in to complete his work.

He inspected the equipment in his usual manner, releasing the bolt a few times to ensure that it was in full working condition. Each time he did it, it was a reminder to those around at that particular moment in time about the consequences of crime. For Pugh, Matthews, and Williams it was a reminder that their time on this Earth was rapidly running out.

The case of Walter Carwardine appeared to reach its impasse. With no one coming forward to provide any more information, the situation was becoming more desperate for his brother, William. He was still looking for answers regarding his brother's final moments and firmly believed that he was murdered. He resorted to producing handbills with the promise of a £20 reward for any information that would lead to a conviction.[9]

Mary Ann Williams had so far kept quiet about her husband's involvement on the night in question. If anything, she had done what was asked of her by providing an alibi for her husband. However, William Williams thought that he and Pugh and Matthews had somehow got away with it. That was until he turned on his wife and beat her furiously in a drunken state. Either through revenge as a means to finally get rid of her husband or through a serious moment of moral reconsideration, she looked at the handbill handed to her.

Mary Ann approached the magistrates with new information that resulted in a new trial. Williams had now revealed that she had not seen her husband all night and when he eventually returned he did so in a flustered state and told to her not to mention anything in case the authorities arrived. It was enough to bring the three men to the Assizes.

Mary Ann stood before the judge and admitted that she had not told the truth at the first trial for fear of reprisals from her husband and the other men involved.[10] She claimed to be around at the time of the murder and the others corroborated her story, including Susan Connop. It was also revealed that the helpful Thomas Pearce, who had claimed to have found Carwardine's hat on the Wye and subsequently helped in the search for his body, was an alias. Thomas Pearce was in fact William Williams.

The other men's alibis were swiftly dismantled as those in the bawdy house that fateful night had also changed their stories. Despite this, the jury still took twenty minutes to reach their verdict, eventually finding Pugh, Matthews, and Williams guilty of murdering Walter Carwardine. For William Carwardine it was a huge victory, but one that eventually saw him in court himself when he failed to pay the reward money to Mary Ann Williams. Williams vs Carwardine proved to be a pivotal case in judicial history as the court ordered him to pay the reward money in 1833.[11]

Pugh and Williams slept soundly on the eve of their execution but the same could not be said about Matthews, who spent his final night crying convulsively throughout the night. The three men continued to plead their innocence even when Burrows arrived to pinion them. Williams stared at the hangman with contempt. Before him stood the man who had previously launched his brother into eternity and now he was about to reunite them. Knowing that in advance, Burrows was wary of what could potentially happen. He entered expecting a confrontation but Williams had already resigned himself to his inevitable fate.

Matthews remained in a state of emotional anguish as he climbed the stairs and when he finally saw three nooses fixed firmly on the crossbeam his legs gave way. He was forced back to his feet and placed above the small crack in the trapdoor. Pugh and Williams remained strong and stared at the crowd below them, maintaining their innocence and urging the crowd to stay away from bad company.

Burrows watched the event before him with little emotion. All he could think about was leaving Hereford and the long journey that awaited him. Nonchalantly, he waited for the signal and pulled the lever, sending the three men to their deaths. Burrows remembered his earlier executions and the excitement of seeing the struggle for life beneath him. Now, after seeing so many falls, it meant nothing to him.

Motionless except for the gentle sway of momentum, Pugh, Matthews, and Williams were dead and Burrows was already looking forward to cutting them down and heading back to Chester. As he descended the platform, he was offered a drink and something to eat. He had an hour to wait before cutting the men down and he would spend it in the gaol. Walking to his room alongside a guard, he was informed that Williams' other brother was also in the gaol for desertion. Perhaps the guard was expecting a reaction from Burrows. Instead, he simply asked what time the coach was coming for him.

Chapter 20

The Swinger Rioters

The Executions of James Lea and Joseph Grindley
Shrewsbury Gaol, 1832

James Cumberledge
New City Gaol, Chester, 1832

JAMES CUMBERLEDGE WAS stewing in the cells at Chester Castle desperately waiting for any news. He was said to have had 'amazing muscular power and stood nearly six feet high',[1] yet the 32-year-old could do nothing about his current predicament. Further inquiries were being conducted after he was found guilty of setting fire to corn stacks at Mr Lea's farm at the Spring Assizes in Chester. Until those inquiries were completed, all he could do was wait.

For Samuel Burrows, it was also out of his hands. As his frustrations grew, he was at least thankful for his payday from Shrewsbury Gaol in order to help finance his latest and ever-longer drinking binges around the public houses of Chester. It was becoming all too familiar for the hangman. The constant waiting despite seeing criminals condemned to death was beginning to create anxiety for him and others in his chosen profession. More and more who were sentenced to death were now gaining respite in the form of alternative punishments and Burrows was wondering if even Cumberledge would slip through his hands like many before him.

There was a faint hope inside Burrows that he would once again tread the boards of his macabre Cestrian theatre once more. The crime that Cumberledge committed was part of something bigger that he had first heard about when he was in Shrewsbury. The men who he executed there only six weeks earlier were dispatched by his hands for a very similar offence, having been condemned as part of the 'Swing Riots' that had taken hold in rural communities.

Much like the Luddites who found their way to his gallows in 1812, the Swing Rioters also held their mythical leader close to their hearts. 'Captain Swing' had replaced Ned Ludd, yet their cause was strikingly similar. The rise of the machines had entered the agricultural fray in the form of the threshing machine. The consequence of this left many farm labourers out of work and in a desperate situation.[2]

Smashing the machines and writing threatening letters, the rioters were also burning crops and corn stacks with the aim of spreading their message to farmers who employed farm labourers. The occurrences began in south-eastern parts of the country and were considered by those in the north to be a faraway problem, but it would not take too long before such incidents came to its door.[3]

It had been an issue facing the country for nearly two years as the Swing Riots continued to gain momentum. With attacks on property still seen as a capital offence, the possibility of the noose still hung over anyone caught carrying out the attacks. Yet there were relatively few executions with regard to the riots. Nineteen people were executed across the country during them, with other forms of punishment largely favoured. Some 505 individuals were transported to the colonies, with a further 644 enduring lengthy prison sentences.[4]

Of the nineteen who were executed, Burrows had already executed two with hopes of a third in the form of James Cumberledge. But now, with some money in his pocket and time on his hands, Burrows' dependence on alcohol was growing dangerously out of hand.

Arriving in Shrewsbury, Burrows stood before the gaol's impressive gate lodge. On the left side of its roof, he could see the completed gallows

The Swinger Rioters

erected for him. He immediately began to think about how much easier it would be to cut down the two men he was about to execute when compared to other places he had been. He smirked with the sheer ease of it all. He did not even have to leave the gaol at all. He just had to simply cut them down and go down a few stairs, then place them in the carts within the safety of the walls. If only other places were as straightforward as this, he thought.

He noticed a bust of a figure on the gatehouse and enquired as to who it was when he was welcomed into the gaol, where he would be staying for the night. For anyone to have a bust for everyone to see, they must be of importance, Burrows thought to himself. He was told that the bust was that of John Howard, the prison reformer who spent his time travelling the country inspecting prisons and improving them. The prison that lay before Burrows was one that he had helped to create alongside William Blackburn and Thomas Telford.[5]

Howard's crusade led to prison reform across the country, even in Chester. Describing Chester Castle on his journeys as like the 'black hole of Calcutta',[6] the old gaol was subsequently redesigned by Thomas Harrison, implementing many of Howard's reforms. Previously, prisoners were held together regardless of their crimes, sex, or age. Debtors were sharing cells with murderers, and both with women and children. Burrows had realised what he had done in asking his question. A brief bit of small talk had somehow turned into a history lesson that he did not want to partake in. Walking behind the gaoler, he had begun to glaze over as the man droned on and on about the gaol itself. At this moment in time, he just wanted his room, some food and, more importantly, something to drink. The talk, however, continued as Burrows was told about the two men he was due to execute the next day. Burrows listened but his attention was beginning to slip away as the gaoler related more details about their crimes.

James Lea and Joseph Grindley were unaware that their executioner had entered the gaol. The two men facing Burrows' noose stared at their cell walls contemplating their impending demise. Given the circumstance that the two men had found themselves in, they had resigned themselves to their upcoming fate.

Following their trial, both men later confessed to their involvement in setting the fires that engulfed John Nunnerley's farm in Whitchurch. Nunnerley was not alone in seeing his crops ablaze following a number of attacks in the area but in the case of Grindley and Lea, it was noted that incendiary balls were used. Some of the balls were found later and when inspected by Thomas Blunt, a local chemist, he declared that his professional opinion was that they could be easily lit and would slowly begin to heat up, allowing the accused to get away before a blaze began. The chemist predicted that it could take fourteen minutes after lighting the balls before a fire started.[7]

Yet Grindley and Lea were not the only ones facing the Shropshire Spring Assizes. Richard Whitfield was also standing before Mr Justice Littledale. He was accused of sending threatening letters to Sir Robert Hill. Found guilty of the offence, Whitfield was spared the noose in favour of transportation.

As Burrows prepared his noose, Grindley's and Lea's time of reckoning had finally arrived. Receiving the sacrament, the two men appeared to be agitated as the end of their lives drew ever closer. Burrows, unfazed by their fear, pinioned the two men in the way that he had done many times before. It had become second nature to him as he nonchalantly carried out his duties with the minimum of fuss despite the continued cries of the men before him. He gazed at Grindley and Lea with a look of disdain as his agricultural upbringing took hold of him. Yet the city had changed him and detached him from their struggles against the changes to the agricultural landscape and the loss of jobs.

As he turned away from the two men, he walked up to the gallows in front of his audience of thousands. Tugging on the rope in order to ensure that it was fully secure, a small cheer was heard. But now was not the time to put on a show. Grindley was the first to ascend the gallows and continued to pray as Burrows placed the noose around his neck. Lea ascended with more difficulty as Burrows and his swaying noose stood before him, yet the fear that he felt somehow allowed him to still walk with a level of impending firmness. Burrows heard Lea's heavy breathing as he placed the hood over him before tightening the noose.[8]

Hearing a mixture of prayer and panic from his latest payday, Burrows' heavy footsteps reverberated around the area as the crowd fell silent. Grindley's prayers filled the vacuum of silence as Burrows' rough hands grabbed the lever. Releasing the bolt, the two men fell. The sound of choking had numbed Burrows as he watched Grindley's and Lea's futile fight for life. As he stared at them, he felt nothing. The thrill that he once felt had evaporated from him as each execution took away his humanity. He used to be proud of what he did and believed fully in the process of law in order to detach himself. Now, he just wanted to go home.

Returning to Chester, Burrows was in a buoyant mood. He hated the constant travel that he felt was being forced upon him. Yet there was something about seeing the familiar places back home that resonated with him. Seeing the cathedral in the distance as his coach approached the city, Burrows breathed a sigh of relief, and the excitement of being home filled him.

With a much-needed payday now behind him, he swiftly turned his attention to the Spring Assizes that were about to take place at Chester Castle. It was the case of James Cumberledge that excited him most as it felt like a carbon copy of the case against the men who he had executed just days ago. Eager to find out more, he decided to head into the public gallery at the Shire Hall to hear exactly what he had done.

Cumberledge was accused of setting fire to corn stacks and other property belonging to Joseph Lea in Siddington, which amounted to a total value of £300. However, there were also differences between the case when compared to the incidents in Whitchurch. There was no physical evidence and, more importantly, no confession.[9]

A long chain of purely circumstantial evidence was put forward by the prosecution but it was enough for the jury to find Cumberledge guilty.

The strength of the case surely meant that Cumberledge would be given a lesser sentence but in making a connection to the previous incendiary fires that had blighted the kingdom over the previous two years, the judge felt it necessary to pass the sentence of death.[10]

Burrows' eyes lit up when he heard the sentence, With the case being so similar to that of Lea and Grindley, he felt sure that this time the sentence would stick. Cumberledge, on the other hand, appeared unaffected, firmly believing that his claim for a pardon would inevitably prevail. His execution date was set for 29 April 1832.

Samuel left the Shire Hall in a good mood and with a date set he began to prepare himself. Seeing the size of Cumberledge, he knew that he needed to get some stronger rope and went in search of it with added enthusiasm. Cumberledge prepared his pardon proceedings and awaited the ruling of the courts.

Cumberledge was given a brief respite as his pardon was being heard. When Burrows was informed he was surprised. After all, it was the same crime that saw him travel to Shrewsbury to complete his work. The notice of respite was read to Cumberledge, which stated that 'further inquiries might be made into his case; great exertions have been made on his behalf, and if any favourable circumstances had been discovered, no doubt they would have had their due weight'.[11] For both Burrows and Cumberledge, it would be an agonising wait.

For twelve days, Cumberledge waited in his cell clinging to the hope that he could be at least transported to Van Diemen's Land. Yet, despite his hope, no one came forward to provide any evidence that could make that possible. Instead, he was informed that his execution date was now set for 12 May. Cumberledge sat in silence and stared at the wall in a state of disbelief. His fate was sealed.

Such was Burrows' infamy across the county of Cheshire, nearly everyone knew who he was. His name appeared in column inches across the county and even further afield, rendering him a bogeyman-like figure. During his younger years, Samuel thrived on his infamy but now as he was approaching his 61st year, it had become a position that gave him less comfort. While he liked being well known, it had brought him little joy with each coming year.

Cumberledge never met Burrows until his infamous date with the hangman but he felt comfortable enough to address him on first-name terms. With religious comfort received, Cumberledge waited for the door of the press room to open. In the doorway stood Burrows armed with rope to pinion the giant who stood before him. As Cumberledge stood up, he towered over Burrows in both height and physical stature. Looking at Cumberledge's thick, muscular arms, Burrows began to think about the worst-case scenario where he might have to fight to pinion the giant that was in front of him. While it was a fight Burrows was more than prepared for, flashes of his ordeal against William Griffith resurfaced. The hangman was getting too old for another fight against a stronger, younger man.

Much to his surprise, Cumberledge did not attempt to fight the hangman. Allowing Burrows to tie up his wrists behind his back, he appeared to have accepted his fate despite his consistent pleas of his innocence. As Samuel left the room, Cumberledge asked him for a favour:

> Now mind, Sam, fetch my carcass as soon as it is done with, though I don't know if it matters much what becomes of my body after it is dead, the soul's all.[12]

Burrows gave a nod but said nothing in return. He could see that the man in front of him was trying to maintain a brave face even though he could hear the fear in his voice. Approaching the steps of the gallows, Cumberledge's steps seemed to falter as the full crowd came into his view. He looked around, seeing the Welsh hills in the distance, and closed his eyes briefly. Looking towards the multitude of the crowd, he was somewhat taken aback by how many people had come to see him die.

Burrows placed the hood over Cumberledge's head before bringing the noose around his neck. There was no showboating from Burrows this time around. Even though he only met Cumberledge briefly, he liked him enough to make sure that this was no spectacle. As he moved away from Cumberledge and walked towards his lever, he could hear the fear in the man's voice once again: 'I am going! Oh! I am going!'[13]

With his hands on the lever, Burrows chose not to wait for Cumberledge to drop his handkerchief. He felt that it was somehow more humane to just put the man out of his misery. Releasing the bolt from underneath Cumberledge, his muscular frame plummeted, breaking his neck, and he died instantly.

Burrows waited an hour before cutting Cumberledge down. Even though he wanted to do it sooner, he knew that he could not as he was legally bound to wait. Despite Cumberledge thinking that his body was worthless, Burrows was instructed to hand it over to a small party of friends so that they could take him back to Siddington for burial.

With his work complete, Samuel walked up Watergate Street, feeling more tired than usual. The events of the day were taking their toll on him as he stared at the cobbled road during his walk home. He was beginning to doubt exactly how much longer he could continue with his work but he also knew that he had little choice but to do so. With finances on a tight budget, and fewer hangings on the horizon, he knew that his choices were limited.

Whenever he stood high above the Cestrian crowd, Samuel looked over the Roodee racecourse, where he could see the smoke steadily rise from the distant house of industry.[14] It was here where the poorest of the poor ended up and, despite its euphemistic, grandiose name, everyone knew exactly what it really was. The workhouse of Chester was a place where no one wanted to end up. Many would prefer Samuel's noose compared to a stint at the workhouse. Each time Samuel saw it, it reminded him why he did his gruesome work. With the cheering crowd beneath him, he kept thinking to himself that he would rather be up above the multitudes on his gallows than making a desperate plea for poor relief. If anything, he felt a slight relief that at least he was not there.

The tiredness had got the better of him by the time he arrived home. Mary, eager to know how his day went, had prepared a meal. But Samuel was too tired to eat. Complaining about feeling poorly, he went to bed. The stew would hold until later as Burrows drifted off into his afternoon slumber.

Chapter 21

The Final Dance of Death

The Executions of Samuel Thorley, John Carr, Thomas Riley, William Naylor and James Mason
New City Gaol, Chester, 1834

IT WAS DUBBED the 'Bloody Assize' by the local newspapers as Burrows chuckled with glee. He was informed that he would be in for a bumper crop in April 1834. Five men were due to face his noose and he was in a celebratory mood. He was not the only one.

The landlords of Chester's public houses were also more than delighted to hear the news. Not only would the city be packed for the event, but they also knew that Samuel Burrows would have the promise of money to part with. Some landlords in the city would often allow Burrows to drink on credit when they knew that he was in for a payday, especially one as large as this, as it allowed them to let the ale flow towards him.[1]

The Old King's Head public house on Lower Bridge Street was a favourite of Burrows precisely for this reason. The landlord, William Challinor,[2] had welcomed Burrows on numerous occasions in the past and news of his bumper payday had soon travelled around town. When Burrows entered the Old King's Head, he was duly welcomed by Challinor. Maintaining a tab, Burrows remained there for the vast majority of the day before eventually moving on.

He would go on to frequent many of Chester's public houses that day, gloating about his next appearance on top of the New City Gaol. For those who firmly believed that Burrows' days were numbered as the city executioner, he was busy promoting his upcoming execution with the same gusto as a ringmaster. It was what the masses actually liked about him. Regardless of his tastelessness, at least he was entertaining in small doses.

Multiple hangings were a worry to many hangmen throughout the county but Burrows had little concern in his inebriated state. In his mind, everything would be fine as he ventured from one end of the city to the other drinking whatever he could. Despite being told to ease up by those watching and eager to place him in the cells, Burrows was quick to sell them the tale that he was OK and would be soon heading home. Entering Northgate Street, he stopped at any place that was still welcoming him. From the Dublin Packet to the Coach & Horses, he then stumbled to The Crown and Mitre before eventually calling it a day and heading home. The short walk back to Brook Street helped to sober him up a little. While he knew that Mary would be wondering where he had been for most of the day, he cared little. One for the road at the Cottage Tavern just a stone's throw away from home wouldn't hurt, and he could continue his pre-execution gloating.

When the morning came, Burrows was worse for wear. Hangovers for the hangman were rare but following the previous day's crawl he was feeling it. The headache grew more intense with every movement as Burrows finally realised where he was. He had been up to his old tricks again and was detained by the authorities on his short walk home. Rather than waking up next to Mary, he was woken by the noises of New City Gaol. Each time this happened the Chester Corporation paid Mr Jepson the cost of boarding Burrows for the night. Mr Jepson, the gaoler of New City Gaol, did not bat an eyelid as the corporation handed him 10 shillings and 10 pence, the nominal fee for anyone detained for being drunk and disorderly.[3] Memories of the pub crawl that he had enjoyed were now blurred, and Burrows desperately tried to sober up. Despite having the first of his five men to execute in the coming hours, his mind was far from the job at hand. Burrows was completely dishevelled and was in no rush to venture to the roof.

The scaffold at New City Gaol had never experienced a four-man execution before and neither was it built with that many in mind. Designed for two condemned persons, the long drop and its trapdoor were faultless. But never before had the weight of four grown men stood on it. In Burrows' arrogant mind, everything would be all right.

A second crossbeam was installed in the belief that that was all that was needed. As Burrows inspected it, he did not see any issues as he was still feeling quite tipsy, he saw no problems. The four men about to drop had no idea that their particular execution would become a circus, with Burrows in the centre stage of the afternoon's calamity.

Of the four men due to face Burrows, there was one in particular whose crime sent shivers down the spines of the Cestrian crowd. James Mason had been dubbed the 'Monster in Human Shape'[4] by many of the local papers and it was a case that the masses simply could not get enough of.

Hannah Woodward had formed an improper relationship with Mason and later it was revealed that she was pregnant with his child. While Mason remained silent regarding the matter, the local parish in Marple had decided to cast Woodwood out. Little did she know that on the Sunday prior to her expulsion, Mason was planning something altogether more sinister.

According to Hannah's own written disposition, the 22-year-old revealed the whole sickening ordeal that she faced at the hands of Mason. In her written account she claimed that she was due to be removed from the parish of Marple to Matlock in Derbyshire. Preparing for the removal, she planned to visit friends just prior to her attack. Making her way to Samuel Martin's home, she spotted Mason and some of his companions on the canal bridge. Hannah wanted little to do with him as she had accepted her move to Matlock in the hope of a fresh start. But Mason had other plans.[5]

Mason dragged Hannah into a nearby wood under the guise of romance and proceeded with his fiendish plan. His aim was to produce a miscarriage of their unborn baby. Mason threw her down to the ground and beat her to an inch of her life. Focusing on her belly, he hoped to kill the baby inside her. Believing that he had achieved his gruesome goal, Mason fled leaving Hannah alone.

Hannah survived her ordeal but such were her wounds and internal bleeding it was inevitable that she would not survive much longer. Amazingly, the baby survived and was born on 25 August 1833. However, Hannah soon sensed that her own life was diminishing. She wrote her account in the hope that it would be used as evidence against Mason in the event of her passing. Hannah Woodward died on 14 January 1834.

Mason was swiftly arrested and tried locally before being sent to Chester Castle to await the Assizes. No witnesses were called in Mason's defence and Hannah's deposition was read aloud to the court. The jury did not take long to return their verdict.

The heinous crime of James Mason would lead him to Burrows' gallows. Judge Baron Gurney laid down the sentence of death, declaring:

> The crime of which you have been convicted is one of the blackest and most atrocious which it has been my misfortune to hear proved in a court of justice. Prepare to meet your God very shortly; it would be cruelty to society to show any mercy to you.[6]

Mason was due to be hanged on 17 April 1834 alongside John Carr, William Naylor, and Thomas Riley, whose crimes were small in comparison. That April was, however, Burrows' busiest to date as before his quadruple execution he also had another date with the drop on 7 April.

Samuel Thorley's name seemed eerily familiar to Cestrians who had heard tales of his great uncle, who was executed on Gallows Hill in 1777 for the murder and subsequent cannibalism of Anne Smith. The two men shared the same name and, ultimately, the same fate as the later Samuel now also awaited the hangman's noose.[7]

Thorley was courting Mary Pemberton. The 21-year-old was living with her recently widowed mother and helped her maintain the farm that was previously run by her father. Thorley was besotted by Mary and promised to marry her, which she gleefully accepted. Yet Thorley was not the man he claimed to be. Promises of their own home never materialised and neither did any preparations for their nuptials. Furthermore, Thorley kept a lot of the darker sides of his life away from his unsuspecting fiancée.

Thorley was a drinker and, much like the man who would eventually execute him, he did this heavily. Soon it was also discovered that Thorley was sleeping around with many women in the town of Northwich and had fathered several illegitimate children. It would not take long until the rumours arrived at the Pemberton farm, whereupon Mary's mother urged her daughter to call off her relationship. After drinking at the Angel Inn, Thorley decided to visit Mary at her home. Perhaps, fearing that their relationship was over if she had heard the swelling rumours about him, he thought he could change her mind or lie his way through the situation.

The two met at the farmhouse. For Mary's mother it was an opportunity for her daughter to end things with Thorley. She opted to leave them alone and retired upstairs. Mary's brother also saw the pair talking but upon his return to the farmhouse, he too went upstairs without sensing any immediate danger.

The front door suddenly slammed. Unsure of what was happening, Mrs Pemberton ventured downstairs to see if Mary had finally ended it with Thorley. Instead, she saw her daughter lying on the floor covered in blood and with her head almost severed from her body.

Thorley ran home, covered in Mary's blood. A servant saw him and Thorley explained what had happened before changing clothes. Rather than wait for the authorities to arrive, he decided to walk to Chester Castle to hand himself in.[8]

With an admission of guilt for the murder of Mary Pemberton, Samuel Thorley had resigned himself to the eventual fate that awaited him as Burrows placed his noose around his neck. It was a simple job for Burrows to complete. He always preferred the ones where the condemned simply gave themselves up to him. Thorley dropped with ease but Burrows knew that the 'Bloody Assizes' was about to give him his toughest job to date.

James Mason, John Carr, William Naylor, and Thomas Riley ascended the gallows slowly as Burrows waited for them on top of New City Gaol. The breeze was refreshing for Burrows and he had hoped that it would keep his hungover head cool from the throbbing headache that had taken over him. When he saw all four men he was trying to solve the puzzle as to how he should place them but with his mind not entirely equipped for the job at hand, he simply wanted to get it over with.

In practice, Burrows had to get the men into their correct positions over the trapdoor. If he had prepared fully before the execution then this would have been a straightforward affair but, still suffering from the previous day's drinking session, thinking straight was not high on his agenda. Placing the men in positions where he just assumed the drop would work, he applied their nooses and awaited the sign to drop them.

Burrows pulled on the lever in the same way that he had done so many times before. This time, however, the bolt wouldn't budge. The weight of all four men combined meant they kept the bolt in place, jarring it against the mechanism. No matter how much Burrows tried pulling on the lever, nothing happened. Soon the hangman experienced something that had never happened to him before as the crowd beneath him began to turn against him. Embarrassed by what was happening, a fretful Burrows quickly began to run around the gallows in a vain attempt to see why the mechanism was failing so spectacularly.[9]

The more he ran around the gallows, the more the crowd laughed at him. Usually, they laughed at his dark comedic attempts to balance on a stool as he flung the rope around the crossbeams, but this was no joke as the four hooded men began to panic, even urinating on the wooden gallows. It took a while for Burrows to realise that the combined weight of the men at the centre of the trapdoor was applying pressure to the bolt that his lever could not release.

Moving them away from the break and alleviating the weight from the bolt, Burrows frantically ran back to his lever. He was angry but as usual took little responsibility for what was happening. How could it possibly be his fault as the crowd continued to laugh in his face. Desperate to get the execution completed, and with sweat streaming from his brow, he gave the lever one last pull.[10]

The four men plummeted this time, clanging together as their momentum took hold. To some, it looked like a gruesome dance as they continued to clatter against each other. The laughter had stopped, and for Burrows the embarrassment was finally over as one by one the souls of the condemned departed their bodies.

George Harrison, the mayor of Chester, was far from impressed by what he witnessed as Burrows had made a hash of the execution. Despite Burrows' pleas that a four-man execution made it harder for him, Harrison was seriously considering relieving Burrows of his duties. Reluctantly, knowing that Burrows was getting older, he allowed him to maintain his position but he was far from impressed as he left the scene. While Samuel was relieved to have kept his job, he had little knowledge that this would be the final time that the masses of Chester would see him at work. With no upcoming executions on the horizon and with his age firmly against him, he knew that his time was effectively up.

The people of Chester would never see him on top of New City Gaol ever again. Their lasting memories of him would be one of a bodged execution as a frantic old man ran desperately around the gallows trying to figure out what to do.

Chapter 22

Fading Away

WHEN SAMUEL AWOKE, he noticed that Mary was perfectly still beside him. Giving her a little nudge, she remained still. His heart raced a little more than usual as he felt the coldness of her body. Mary had passed away in the night as the two slept without as much as a whimper. Sam knew that she went peacefully. It was the smallest of consolation as his emotions ran high. The tears streamed down his face as he sobbed. Despite her being ill for the latter part of 1834 and into 1835, he never thought that she would actually leave him.

His mind ventured back to the happier times of their relationship. Their first meeting, their wedding day, the time when she fought so hard to find him when the press gang arrived for him, seeing her playing with Henry and Charles and the tender moments they all shared together. He remembered her laugh, her radiant smile but also the disapproving frown she displayed whenever he did anything wrong, which had grown in frequency. He loved every part of her and now she was gone. He cradled her lifeless body and looked up to the heavens, pleading for the Lord to take care of her.

Now, the guilt began to consume him. He regretted not spending enough time with her as he gave in to his own selfish desires. The drink took over in the later years of their relationship and his own vanity with his position as the city executioner slowly faded from relevance.

Samuel had looked after Mary as best as he possibly could as her illness slowly took over but prior to that he had not given her too much thought. In 1834, his own pleasure far exceeded that of his wife. It was a pleasure that had got him into a series of problems with the law in Chester.

Drinking to excess in order to forget about what was happening around him would be his typical excuse, but on the whole he secretly enjoyed being in his inebriated state.

Throughout 1834, Sammy was firmly on the radar of the authorities as his drinking continued to get him into trouble. Mary chose to ignore his antics as she chose to suffer in relative silence. Their relationship had never fully recovered since Charles was sent to Van Diemen's Land and with the never-releasing grip of grief following the death of Henry, the two became tolerant of each other for survival. Mary was not one to be a burden to her husband, opting to play the role of a background actor in the story of his life. Sammy was the star and he made sure everyone knew that.

With his days as Chester's executioner drawing to a close, Burrows was still holding out hope that he would still be of use, especially after such a formidable start to the year. Following the executions of Samuel Thorley, John Carr, Thomas Riley, William Naylor, and of course, the now infamous James Mason, Burrows continued to act as if he still held some importance within Cestrian circles, even though he secretly knew that his age was now firmly against him.

Despite his bumper haul, Burrows knew that Mary was unwell. At seven years his senior, he realised that if he was feeling his years, then Mary would be also. The loving husband was a role that never quite suited Samuel. Instead, he required someone who would just put up with his antics as time went on. In that respect, Mary was his doting wife. With money in his pocket following his five executions, Burrows swiftly got into trouble.

On 14 August 1834, he found himself in a cell at the very gaol where he once walked through with a level of confidence and esteem as his footsteps echoed around the cells. He was charged with breaking the peace in the City of Chester and incarcerated among those who he despised most. He would be discharged by the mayor on 3 September on the grounds of his previous work for the authorities of Chester. However, it would not take long before Burrows found himself in trouble once again.[1]

Fading Away

He was back in the cells once again on 13 September and this time he was charged with assaulting William Darlington. This time around, Burrows would spend a longer time in the confines of New City Gaol, eventually being discharged on 22 October.[2] By all accounts, Burrows pleaded that he would never get in trouble again and never did.

His final potential execution once again slipped through his fingers in the way many did previously. However, in the case of James Garside and Joseph Mosley, it was because the Chester Corporation had grown tired of its responsibility for executing those within the county. In the case of Garside and Mosley, Chester simply refused to execute them, suggesting that their role in the macabre proceedings was simply becoming too much and too expensive. Aggrieved by the nature of their calling since Henry VII's Great Charter, the city was now beginning to flex its muscles in order to get more compensation from the crown. For Burrows, it was a disaster. In his mind, his career was all but over.[3]

With Mary getting worse, Burrows decided that he would keep away from the main streets, where he had now become a menace. Instead, he mainly kept himself to the Gorse Stacks area of Chester, helping and comforting Mary as her condition worsened.

Mary Burrows died aged 70 in March 1835 and Samuel was helpless without her. While the couple made sure they had saved enough to ensure a burial, Burrows was now reduced to his retainer and rat-catching income. There were no further executions on the horizon and Burrows became a more frequent visitor to the local public houses around him, including the Cottage Tavern, ensuring that his drunken walk home was more reachable.

He had carried out Mary's wishes, making sure that she was buried in the churchyard of St Oswald's on the south transept of Chester Cathedral.[4] This had been their church ever since they had met. It was where Burrows performed his duties as a beadle, where their children were baptised, and where they attended Sunday services. It had become an important part of their lives and in death it was to be their final resting place. Burrows wanted to be buried next to her when his time came. Little did he know just how soon it would be.

The Noose of Samuel Burrows

Just seven months later, after a period of heavy drinking, Burrows had succeeded in doing enough damage to himself to bring him to the point of death. As he retold stories of his glory days to anyone interested enough to listen, Burrows drank himself to death safe in the knowledge that the authorities had now taken less interest in him. He yearned for Mary's disapproving looks, but with no one to chastise him his self-destructive nature was given free rein.

His conversations in the final weeks of his life with Reverend William Clarke had slowly begun to have an effect on him. Despite telling Clarke his many stories, he had at least begun to show some remorse for what he had done. His body was slowly dying, but he cared little for his earthly body. He just wanted to be gone and reunited with Mary, who he knew would be in heaven. He prayed that his attempts to salvage his own soul with the help of Reverend Clarke would work for him.

Reverend Clarke arrived to find Samuel Burrows dead.[5] He had left him briefly as he checked on him after Burrows had asked for some sustenance. Clarke went to fetch some cheese, bread, and ale but on his return it was too late. It had just gone four o'clock in the afternoon as Clarke stared at the departed Burrows with neither a feeling of sorrow nor relief. Instead, he had prepared himself for this moment in the knowledge that the hangman was running out of time. A Bible was beside him and opened as if it was the final thing that Burrows read before his soul departed from his earthly body.

Clarke sat on the bed beside Burrows and picked up the Bible. He noticed that Burrows was reading the gospel of John and had highlighted a certain passage. John Chapter 11, verses 25–26, was underlined, which states: 'Jesus said to her, "I am the resurrection and the life. The one who believes in me will live, even though they die; and whoever lives by believing in me will never die."'

Somehow, he had got through to the hangman, who was begging for salvation in the final moments of his life. Clarke breathed a sigh of relief. It had restored his faith that all men could be saved. He took a moment, recomposed himself, and then headed out to report Burrows' death so that his body could be removed. Knowing that his final request was to be buried by his wife at St Oswald's, Clarke felt that it was only right to fulfil his dying wish.[6]

Burrows had saved enough money in order to ensure that he would be buried and Clarke made sure that all preparations were completed. Clarke then made his way to Handbridge to the printers W. Byrne in order to finalise the broadside entitled 'The Conversion and Death of Samuel Burrows'. The author is unknown but it is plausible that it was written by Clarke alongside Burrows. As he read through the piece he gave the printers a nod, although he was still unsure of what was actually true. It was what Burrows wanted after all. This one-page broadside was his story, no matter what had been embellished or even censored.

Samuel Burrows still remained an enigma to Clarke. Some of what was written in his broadside he knew was far from true. If anything, it presented a well-meaning man who believed in what he did but through their conversations and with what Clarke already knew about the infamous hangman, he knew that the document about to be distributed was largely a case of smoke and mirrors. Either way, given how the newspapers had already wrongly declared Burrows to be already dead, Clarke made it his mission to let Chester know that he was now officially gone.

Burrows was buried three days later on 23 October 1835 at a small service performed by J. Boydell that only a few people attended. Clarke looked around and saw life continue around him on the busy Chester streets. He had previously read a passage about Burrows' death that declared 'Death of an Important Personage'.[7] He knew that Burrows would have liked that; if anything, Clarke thought that perhaps Burrows might have even written it himself.

However, this opinion of Burrows was not shared by everyone. *The Chester Courant*, which had previously declared that Burrows was dead while he was still very much alive, published a scathing obituary. It read:

> Sammy Burrows, the well-known finisher of the law … was, by definition, not only a pig-killer, a rat-killer, a mole-killer and a man-killer, but also a self-destructive, for by all accounts, he killed himself with ardent drink, which produced a serious complaint of the liver. We are creditably informed, that such was the obduracy of this man's feeling, occasioned by the execution of about 50 criminals, that he never heard of the probability of a hanging matter without calculating on the profits which would be awarded him. In many instances, he was known to drink the amount of his wages on credit, before the execution took place.[8]

Even in death, Burrows was still being talked about and while some aimed to find some positives about him, others were quick to remind Cestrians about who he really was regardless of his final moments of repentance. What is certain though, is that Chester would never experience an individual like him high above the New City Gaol again.

Samuel Burrows would be the last to hold the position of Chester's hangman. Following his death, the authorities opted not to open the position to others. Instead, Chester would invite visiting hangmen to the city in order to complete public executions until the practice was outlawed in 1868. Following Burrows' death, there would only be nine more public executions in Chester, performed by the likes of William Calcraft, George Smith, and William Marwood.[9]

As the era of public executions faded from public memory, so did Burrows. For a man who believed in his own importance and indeed the importance of the service that he provided, it did not take long for people to move on. Soon his memory faded into the ether and was relegated to the confines of the archives.

Fading Away

Burrows experienced a period of great change and revolt during his lifetime. Most of the crimes committed by those that he executed were a product of that change, ranging from the impact of the industrial and agricultural revolutions to the impact felt by many during the Napoleonic Wars and the cost to the country that they imposed. Desperation and the impact of economic recessions and inflation saw many resort to criminal activity at a time when fear of revolution was severely controlled by the noose. When reform eventually came, Burrows became the victim of a system that was once previously lucrative. While he believed that criminals should face the ultimate sanction, successive governments instead phased out the role of public executions in favour of transportation.

Chester's memory continues to fade further. Over time, histories would be written often excluding the likes of Burrows and even the victims who stood on the gallows high above the Cestrian crowds. Yet these lives are important to help our understanding, not only of everyday life in Georgian England, or even in the history of crime and punishment, but to also remind us that the noose of Samuel Burrows itself had a story to tell.

Notes

Chapter 1: The Hangman's Burden

1. Yarwood, Derek, *Cheshire's Execution Files*, p.89.
2. *The Chester Courant*, 26 August 1826.
3. Ibid.
4. Charles Burrows was sentenced to transportation to Van Diemen's Land on 12 April 1824 for stealing stockings. Chester Gaol Registers 1808–1865 (ZQAQ/3 Cheshire Record Office).
5. Yarwood, Derek, *Cheshire's Execution Files*, p.89. The reference is a rough estimate of how many criminals Burrows was believed to have executed but given his travelling around parts of the country this is on the lower side.
6. Much of the information here comes from the broadside 'The Conversion and Death of Samuel Burrows', which has been reproduced in Yarwood, Derek, *Cheshire's Execution Files*. It states how Reverend W. Clarke was on hand to provide spiritual guidance as Burrows was slowly dying in Brook Street.
7. Reverend W. Clarke held a number of positions within the city, including New City Gaol and St John's Hospital.

Chapter 2: Life Before the Noose

1. There are numerous examples of Samuel Burrows getting in trouble with the law, which can be found in both of Chester's local newspapers

Notes

(*The Chester Courant* and *Chester Chronicle*) as well as Chester Gaol Registers 1808–1865 (ZQAQ/3 Cheshire Record Office).
2. 'The Conversion and Death of Samuel Burrows'.
3. Diocese of Chester Parish Register of Marriages c.1538–1910. Samuel signs his name, proving a certain level of education. Mary Williams marks her name with a cross.
4. *A History of the County of Chester: Volume 5 Part 1, The City of Chester: General History and Topography*. Originally published by Victoria County History, London, 2003. British History Online, Institute of Historical Research.
5. Samuel Burrows was highlighted as a parish beadle in a number of sources including Hutchinson, J.R., *The Press-Gang: Afloat and Ashore*, (E.P. Dutton & Co., 1914), p.251.
6. Champness, John, *Thomas Harrison Georgian Architect of Chester and Lancaster, 1744–1829* (University of Lancaster, 2005).
7. Executions at Northgate Gaol highlighted on https://chester.shoutwiki.com/wiki/Execution_at_Chester
8. Yarwood, Derek, *Cheshire's Execution Files*, p.94.

Chapter 3: The Men Who Hanged Twice

1. It had been eight years since Chester hosted a public execution, with the last being in 1801 in which Aaron Gee and Thomas Gibson were executed at Northgate Gaol for the uttering of counterfeit bank notes.
2. The New City Gaol was completed in 1807, with inmates being transferred from Northgate Gaol soon after.
3. The Chester City Gaol is often said to be one of the first to install a 'drop', or mechanical gallows. https://chester.shoutwiki.com/wiki/Execution_at_Chester
4. The Tale of John Clare is best told by Dark Chester's tour guide David Atkinson. YouTube: Chester Heritage Festival, Dark Chester – The Tale of John Clare.

5. *A History of the County of Chester: Volume 5 Part 1, The City of Chester: General History and Topography*. Originally published by Victoria County History, London, 2003. British History Online, Institute of Historical Research.
6. Comprehensive detail of the Woolpack Inn, https://chesterwalls.info/woolpack.html
7. Yarwood, Derek, *Cheshire's Execution Files*, pp.135–136.
8. Wade, Stephen, *Britain's Most Notorious Hangmen*, Chapter 7, Samuel Burrows.
9. Walliss, John, *Crime and Justice in Georgian Cheshire: The Chester Court of Great Sessions, 1760–1830* (Journal of European History of Law Vol. 6/ 2015 No. 1), p.47.
10. *Chester Courant*, 12 May 1809.
11. Hurren, Elizabeth: *Dissecting the Criminal Corpse: Staging Post-Execution Punishment in Early Modern England*, p.81.
12. Ibid.
13. *Chester Courant*, 12 May 1809.
14. 'A Walk on the Darker Side of Vale Royal', *Warrington Guardian*, 24 October 2001.

Chapter 4: A Done Deal

1. Williams, M.R. (2001). Rowlands, Griffith (1761–1828), surgeon. *Dictionary of Welsh Biography*. Retrieved 21 July 2024, from https://biography.wales/article/s3-ROWL-GRI-1761
2. Ibid.
3. *Lancaster Gazette*, 12 May 1810.
4. Ibid.
5. Ibid.
6. *The Sun* (London), 7 May 1810.
7. Tarlow, Sarah & Battell Lowman, Emma, *Harnessing the Power of the Criminal Corpse*, pp.87–88.

Notes

Chapter 5: Rage Against the Machines

1. Cheshire Special Commission, 25 May 1812. A Calendar of the Criminal Prisoners in the Custody of Matthew Hudson, Constable of His Majesty's Gaol, The Castle of Chester (HO 42/123 National Archives).
2. The Fourth Report of the Committee of the Society for the Improvement of Prison Discipline and the Reformation of Juvenile Offenders.
3. Cheshire Special Commission, 25 May 1812. A Calendar of the Criminal Prisoners in the Custody of Matthew Hudson, Constable of His Majesty's Gaol, The Castle of Chester (HO 42/123 National Archives).
4. Ibid.
5. Ibid.
6. Ibid.
7. The Luddite Bicentenary 1811–1817. This website includes a number of primary sources, including newspaper reports, posters, letters and reports. https://udditebicentenary.blogspot.com/2012/04/4th-april-1812-rising-tensions-in.html
8. *The Philanthropist, Or, Repository for Hints and Suggestions Calculated to Promote the Comfort and Happiness of Man: Volume 2*, p.316.
9. The Luddite Bicentenary 1811–1817. https://udditebicentenary.blogspot.com/2012/04/4th-april-1812-rising-tensions-in.html
10. Reward poster for arson at William Radcliffe's warehouse (HO 40/1/1 National Archives).
11. https://udditebicentenary.blogspot.com/2012/04/14th-april-1812-rioting-loom-breaking.html
12. Cheshire Special Commission, 25 May 1812. A Calendar of the Criminal Prisoners in the Custody of Matthew Hudson, Constable of His Majesty's Gaol, The Castle of Chester (HO 42/123 National Archives).
13. Sale, Kirkpatrick, *Rebels Against The Future: The Luddites And Their War On The Industrial Revolution: Lessons For The Computer Age*, p.132.

14. Cheshire Special Commission, 25 May 1812. A Calendar of the Criminal Prisoners in the Custody of Matthew Hudson, Constable of His Majesty's Gaol, The Castle of Chester (HO 42/123 National Archives).
15. Ibid.
16. *Chester Courant*, 16 June 1812.
17. Details of Burrows' stature can be found in his description following his arrest. Chester Gaol Registers 1808–1865 (ZQAQ/3 Cheshire Record Office).
18. Wade, Stephen, *Britain's Most Notorious Hangmen*, Chapter 7.
19. *Chester Chronicle*, 16 June 1812.

Chapter 6: A Very Public Ordeal

1. Nield, Maureen, *Rope Dance: A Sensational Murder in Regency Cheshire Re-opened*, pp.7–10.
2. *The Sun* (London), 27 August 1812.
3. The Testimony of Hannah Evans. The Trial at Large of John Lomas and Edith Morrey for Petit Treason … at Chester … the 21st Day of August 1812 (207013 Cheshire Record Office).
4. Nield, Maureen, *Rope Dance: A Sensational Murder in Regency Cheshire Re-opened*, pp.14–15.
5. Ibid., p.20.
6. Ibid., p.47.
7. Ibid.
8. Ibid.
9. Lomas's Letter to his Father, pp.70–71.
10. Ibid., p.49.
11. Ibid., pp. 50–51.
12. Teddy Bock, a cryer of dying speeches (woodcut), appears in Nield, Maureen, *Rope Dance: A Sensational Murder in Regency Cheshire Re-opened*, p.52.

Notes

13. 'John Lomas's Sorrowful Lamentation and Last Farewell to the World'. Re-published in Nield, Maureen, *Rope Dance: A Sensational Murder in Regency Cheshire Re-opened*, p.73.
14. Ibid.
15. Nield, Maureen, *Rope Dance: A Sensational Murder in Regency Cheshire Re-opened*, p.51.
16. Death Warrant of John Lomas & Edith Morrey (QAB 5/8/9 Cheshire Record Office).
17. Phillipson, Tacye, *Anatomy: A Matter of Death and Life*, p.93.
18. Nield, Maureen, *Rope Dance: A Sensational Murder in Regency Cheshire Re-opened*, p.51.
19. Ibid., p.65.
20. Yarwood, Derek, *Cheshire's Execution Files*, p.98.
21. Ibid., p.59.
22. Ibid., pp.60–61.

Chapter 7: The Tragedy of Miss Porter

1. *A History of the County of Chester: Volume 5 Part 1, The City of Chester: General History and Topography*. Originally published by Victoria County History, London, 2003. British History Online, Institute of Historical Research.
2. Wood, Chris, *Famous Last Words: Confessions, Humour and Bravery of the Departing.* (Chapter 18).
3. Ibid.
4. *Chester Chronicle*, 30 April 1813.
5. Ibid.
6. Yarwood, Derek, *Cheshire's Execution Files*, p.99.
7. Wood, Chris, *Famous Last Words: Confessions, Humour and Bravery of the Departing.* (Chapter 18).
8. Ibid.
9. Ibid.

10. Ibid.
11. *Lancaster Gazette*, 3 July 1813.

Chapter 8: This Time It's Personal

1. Broadside detailing the execution of William Wilson 1814 (231588 Cheshire Record Office).
2. Crime and Punishment in Chester (Chester Records Office).
3. Hutchinson, J.R., *The Press-Gang: Afloat and Ashore*, p.251.
4. Ibid., pp.251–252.
5. Ibid., p.252.
6. Ibid., p.220.
7. Broadside detailing the execution of William Wilson 1814 (231588 Cheshire Record Office).
8. 'The examination of Samuels Burrowes at the City of Chester, Butcher, Late Beadle of the said City and Mary, his wife'. Admiralty and Ministry of Defence, Navy Department: Correspondence and Papers. Letters from Captains, Surname B. Folios 185–186. William Birchall. (ADM 1/1532/101A National Archives).
9. Ibid.
10. Ibid.
11. Ibid.
12. https://chester.shoutwiki.com/wiki/Grosvenor_Museum. For more information regarding 'The Honourable Incorporation of the King's Arms Kitchen', consult Steve Howe's excellent virtual tour of Chester https://chesterwalls.info
13. Broadside detailing the execution of William Wilson 1814 (231588 Cheshire Record Office).
14. Ibid.
15. Reports on criminals: correspondence: Report of W. Garrows on 1 individual petition (Matthew Hudson) on behalf of William Wilson. (HO 47/53/17 National Archives).

Notes

16. *Chester Courant*, 30 May 1814.
17. Ibid.
18. Ibid.

Chapter 9: The Devil's Bank Notes

1. Roberts, Matthew, *Satan's Bank Note* (History Today, September 2017).
2. Ibid.
3. Broadside describing the fate of Joseph Allen (231596 Cheshire Records Office).
4. McGowen, Randell, *Managing the Gallows: The Bank of England and the Death Penalty, 1797–1821*, pp.241–282.
5. Ibid.
6. Prisoners' Letters to the Bank of England, 1781–1827 [F25/1/145] Thomas Rushton, Giltspur Street Compter, 13 May 1802.
7. https://convictrecords.com.au/convicts/rushton/thomas/108333
8. McGowen, Randell, *Managing the Gallows: The Bank of England and the Death Penalty, 1797–1821*, p.282.
9. Yarwood, Derek, *Cheshire's Execution Files*, p.123.
10. Broadside describing the fate of Joseph Allen (231596 Cheshire Records Office).
11. Yarwood, Derek, *Cheshire's Execution Files*, p.121.
12. Broadside describing the fate of Joseph Allen (231596 Cheshire Records Office).
13. *Chester Chronicle*, 2 May 1817.
14. www.regencyhistory.net/blog/1816-year-without-sumhttps://www.regencyhistory.net/blog/1816-year-without-summermer
15. Broadside describing the fate of Joseph Allen (231596 Cheshire Records Office).
16. *Chester Chronicle*, 2 May 1817.
17. Hurley, Paul, 'Market trader paid the ultimate price for forging bank notes', *Knutsford Guardian*, 22 August 2021.

Chapter 10: The Road to Near Ruin

1. *Chester Chronicle*, 22 September 1820.
2. *English Chronicle* and *Whitehall Evening Post*, 23 September 1823.
3. Hughes, Thomas, *The Stranger's Handbook to Chester and its Environs*, pp.80–81.
4. 33–37 Clwyd Street, Ruthin is now a flower shop but was previously the Red Lion Inn where Burrows stayed the evening prior to the execution of John Connor, https://www.peoplescollection.wales/items/33738#?xywh=-53%2C-1%2C4105%2C2456
5. Jones, John, a/ac John Jones. *Can newydd yn rhoddi hanes John Connor, Gwyddel 32 oed, yr hwn a ddienyddiwyd yn Rhuthun, Llun 15 Ebrill 1822, am yspeilio ac ymgais llofruddio, ar y ffordd rhwng Gwrecsam a Marchwiail/J. Jones, Treffynnon*. Trefriw: Argraffwyd gan J. Jones, 1822. Print. (The National Library of Wales).
6. www.peoplescollection.wales/items/33738#?xywh=-53%2C-1%2C4105%2C2456
7. *The Sun* (London), 20 April 1822.

Chapter 11: Five Days Racing and a Hanging

1. Chester Gaol Registers 1808–1865 (ZQAQ/3 Cheshire Record Office).
2. Peter Crawley, Pioneer bare-knuckle boxer, nicknamed 'Rumpsteak' and 'Young Rump Steak', whose trade was a meat butcher.
3. Peter Crawley vs Southern's Bully. Crawley Victory on 7 May 1822 in Chester.
4. Yarwood, Derek, *Cheshire's Execution Files*, p.161.
5. *London Packet* and *New Lloyd's Evening Post*, 13 May 1822.
6. Ibid.

Notes

Chapter 12: On the Road Again

1. *Chester Chronicle*, 3 January 1823. Burrows was arrested in 1822 but waited in Chester Castle for the next Assizes.
2. Gatrell, Vic, *The Hanging Tree: Execution and the English People*, p.422.
3. *Glasgow Sentinel*, 2 October 1822.
4. Griffith, Owen, a/ac John Jones. *Cerdd alarus, yn rhoddi hanes am Lewis Owen, yr hwn a ddienyddwyd ar Forfa Seiont, gerllaw Caerynarfon, ar ddydd Mercher Medi 4ydd, 1822 : efe a garcharwyd am amcan lladd Mr. Sturdy (Supervisor), Conwy ... Cenir ar 'Fryniau'r Iwereddon/ [gan] Owain ap Cyffin, Migmint ; Meirion, a'i cant.* Llanrwst: Argraffwyd John Jones, 1825. Print. (The National Library of Wales).
5. Ibid.
6. *Glasgow Sentinel*, 2 October 1822.
7. Ibid.

Chapter 13: Dead Man's Clothes

1. Yarwood, Derek, *Cheshire's Execution Files*, p.103.
2. Leigh J., *Trial, Conviction and Execution of Samuel Fallowes, for the Wilful Murder of Betty Shawcross: Before Chief Justice Warren & Serjt Marshall, at Chester on Friday, April 11, 1823*, p.27.
3. Yarwood, Derek, *Cheshire's Execution Files*, p.165.
4. Ibid., p.167.
5. Ibid., p.168.
6. Leigh J., *Trial, Conviction and Execution of Samuel Fallowes, for the Wilful Murder of Betty Shawcross: Before Chief Justice Warren & Serjt Marshall, at Chester on Friday, April 11, 1823*, p.3.
7. Ibid.
8. Ibid., p.5.
9. Ibid., p.9.
10. Ibid., p.11.

11. Ibid., p.21.
12. Ibid., pp.23–24.
13. Ibid.
14. Yarwood, Derek, *Cheshire's Execution Files*, p.185.
15. Leigh J., *Trial, Conviction and Execution of Samuel Fallowes, for the Wilful Murder of Betty Shawcross: Before Chief Justice Warren & Serjt Marshall, at Chester on Friday, April 11, 1823*, p.26.
16. Ibid., p.27.
17. Ibid.

Chapter 14: The Changing Tide

1. *Chester Courant*, 15 April 1823.
2. Ibid.
3. Ibid.
4. Ibid.
5. Ibid.
6. Ibid.
7. Devereaux, Simon, *Execution, State and Society in England, 1660–1900,* Chapter 8, The 'Bloody Code' Diminished, 1822–1830.
8. Ibid.
9. Ibid.
10. Hughes, Thomas, *The Stranger's Handbook to Chester and its Environs*, pp.80–81.
11. *A History of the County of Chester: Volume 5 Part 2, The City of Chester: Culture, Buildings, Institutions.* Originally published by Victoria County History, London, 2003. British History Online, Institute of Historical Research.
12. The Judgement of Death Act 1823.
    'That from and after the passing of this Act, whenever any Persons shall be convicted of any Felony, except Murder, and shall by Law be excluded the Benefit of Clergy in respect thereof, and the Court

before which such Offender shall be convicted shall be of Opinion that, under the particular Circumstances of the case, such Offender is a fit and proper Subject to be recommended for the Royal Mercy, it shall and may be lawful for such Court, if it shall think fit so to do, to direct the proper Officer then being present in Court to require and ask, whereupon such Officer shall require and ask, if such Offender hath or knoweth any thing to say why Judgment of Death should not be recorded against such Offender; and in case such Offender shall not allege any Matter or Thing sufficient in Law to arrest or bar such Judgment, the Court shall and may and is hereby authorized to abstain from pronouncing Judgment of Death upon such Offender; and instead of pronouncing such Judgment to order the same to be entered of Record, and thereupon such proper Officer as aforesaid shall and may and is hereby authorized to enter Judgment of Death on Record against such Offender, in the usual and accustomed Form, and in such and the same Manner as is now used, and as if Judgment of Death had actually been pronounced in open Court against such Offender, by the Court before which such Offender shall have been convicted.'

Chapter 15: The Curious Case of Charles Burrows

1. 'The Conversion and Death of Samuel Burrows' has been reproduced in Yarwood, Derek, *Cheshire's Execution Files*.
2. *Chester Chronicle*, 3 January 1823.
3. *Chester Chronicle*, 23 January 1824.
4. *Chester Courant*, 20 April 1824.
5. 'The Conversion and Death of Samuel Burrows' has been reproduced in Yarwood, Derek, *Cheshire's Execution Files*.
6. *Chester Courant*, 20 April 1824.
7. Charles Burrows was sentenced to transportation to Van Diemen's Land on 12 April 1824 for stealing stockings. Chester Gaol Registers 1808–1865 (ZQAQ/3 Cheshire Record Office).

8. www.naomiclifford.com/justitia-prison-hulk-woolwich
9. Muster Roll from *Princess Charlotte* for convict Charles Burrows (CON 13/1/3 p.109, Tasmania Libraries).
10. Medical Journal of the *Princess Charlotte*, Convict Ship from 12 June to 1 December 1824. (National Archives ADM 101/61/6).
11. Alexander, Alison, *Tasmania's Convicts: How Felons Built A Free Society*, p.8.
12. Description List of Convicts, Charles Burrows (CON 23/1/1 No 775, Tasmania Libraries).
13. Ibid.
14. Convict Conduct Record, Charles Burrows (CON 31/1/1, Tasmania Libraries).

Chapter 16: The Hangman's Idle Hands

1. *Pigot and Co.'s Commercial Directory for Cheshire 1822–23*.
2. Ibid.
3. *Chester Chronicle*, 31 March 1826.
4. *Chester Chronicle*, 9 September 1825.
5. Ibid.
6. Ibid.
7. *Chester Chronicle*, 31 March 1826.
8. Ibid.
9. Ibid.

Chapter 17: Tears of the Hangman

1. Broadside detailing the executions of Joseph Woodhouse and John Henshall 1829 (231594 Cheshire Record Office).
2. Ibid.
3. *Chester Chronicle*, 2 October 1829.

4. Ibid.
5. Wade, Stephen, *Britain's Most Notorious Hangmen*, Chapter 7, Samuel Burrows.
6. *Chester Chronicle*, 2 October 1829.
7. Ibid.
8. Broadside detailing the executions of Joseph Woodhouse and John Henshall 1829 (231594 Cheshire Record Office).
9. *Manchester Chronicle*, 3 October 1829.

Chapter 18: When the Hangman Came to Beaumaris

1. Hughes, Margaret, *Crime and Punishment at Beaumaris*, p.73.
2. Ibid., p.74.
3. *Pigot and Co.'s Commercial Directory for Cheshire 1828–29*.
4. www.capitalpunishmentuk.org/beaumaris.html
5. Ibid.
6. *North Wales Chronicle*, September 1830.
7. www.anglesey-history.co.uk
8. *The Sun* (London), 18 September 1830.
9. Ibid.
10. Final resting place of William Griffith by the wall inside of the gaol. He is buried alongside Richard Rowlands, who was executed in 1862 by William Calcraft.

Chapter 19: The Hat on the Wye

1. Sly, Nicola, *Herefordshire Murders*, Chapter 3.
2. Ibid.
3. 'Broadside: A particular account of the trial and execution of William Williams, John Matthews, and Joseph Pugh, who suffered this day, Monday, March 26th, 1832, on the drop in front of the County Gaol,

in the City of Hereford, for the murder of Walter Carwardine, on the night of Thursday, the 24th of March, 1831', Kent State University Libraries. Special Collections and Archives.
4. Ibid.
5. Sly, Nicola, *Herefordshire Murders*, Chapter 3.
6. *Hereford Journal*, 21 April 1830.
7. Sly, Nicola, *Herefordshire Murders*, Chapter 3.
8. Ibid.
9. Williams v Carwardine [1833] EWHC KB J44 (22 March 1833).
10. *The Sun* (London), 28 March 1832.
11. Williams v Carwardine [1833] EWHC KB J44 (22 March 1833).

Chapter 20: The Swinger Rioters

1. *Englishman*, 27 May 1832.
2. https://blogs.kent.ac.uk/ageofrevolution/riots/the-swing-riots
3. Ibid.
4. Former Her Majesty's Prison, Shrewsbury, www.historicengland.org.uk
5. What caused the 'Swing Riots' in the 1830s?, www.nationalarchives.gov.uk
6. www.prisonhistory.org/lockup/chester-castle
7. *A Narrative of the Fires Which Occurred In the Parish of Whitchurch, Shropshire, In the Years 1830 And 1831: Together With an Account of the Trials of James Lea And Joseph Grindley, Etc*. Whitchurch: H. Newling, 1832, pp.23–49.
8. *English Chronicle and Whitehall Evening Post*, 7 April 1832.
9. Broadside describing the Trial and Execution of James Cumberledge (231590 Cheshire Records Office).
10. Ibid.
11. Ibid.
12. Ibid.
13. Ibid.
14. The House of industry was situated on Kitchen Street near the racecourse before a new workhouse was erected in Hoole in 1878.

Chapter 21: The Final Dance of Death

1. Yarwood, Derek, *Cheshire's Execution Files*, p.93.
2. *Pigot and Co.'s Commercial Directory for Cheshire 1828–29.*
3. Yarwood, Derek, *Cheshire's Execution Files*, p.103.
4. Executions of criminals: more generally known by the uninviting name of 'Dying speeches'. Execution broadside (James Mason) (Harvard University, 1834).
5. Ibid.
6. Ibid.
7. Did Murder Run in the Family? (Paul Hurley, *Northwich Guardian*, 24 January 2021).
8. Ibid.
9. Yarwood, Derek, *Cheshire's Execution Files*, p.102.
10. Ibid.

Chapter 22: Fading Away

1. Chester Gaol Registers 1808–1865 (ZQAQ/3 Cheshire Record Office).
2. Ibid.
3. Yarwood, Derek, *Cheshire's Execution Files*, p.93.
4. Burials at St Oswalds 1833–1839 (MF 108/9 Cheshire Records Office).
5. *Chester Chronicle*, 23 October 1835.
6. Burials at St Oswalds 1833–1839 (MF 108/9 Cheshire Records Office).
7. *Chester Chronicle*, 23 October 1835.
8. Yarwood, Derek, *Cheshire's Execution Files*, p.93.
9. https://chester.shoutwiki.com/wiki/Execution_at_Chester

Bibliography

Archival Sources

Admiralty and Ministry of Defence, Navy Department: Correspondence and Papers. Letters from Captains, Surname B. Folios 182–183. William Birchall. (ADM 1/1532/101A National Archives).

Admiralty and Ministry of Defence, Navy Department: Correspondence and Papers. Letters from Captains, Surname B. Folios 186–187. William Birchall. (ADM 1/1532/101A National Archives).

Broadside detailing the execution of William Wilson 1814 (231588 Cheshire Record Office).

Broadside detailing the executions of Joseph Woodhouse and John Henshall 1829 (231594 Cheshire Record Office).

Broadside describing the fate of Joseph Allen (231596 Cheshire Records Office).

Broadside describing the trial and execution of James Cumberledge (231590 Cheshire Records Office).

Broadside detailing the trial, conviction and execution of Samuel Fallows (Folder 5 (33) John Johnson Collection, Bodleian Library, University of Oxford).

Broadside: A particular account of the trial and execution of William Williams, John Matthews, and Joseph Pugh, who suffered this day, Monday, March 26th, 1832, on the drop in front of the County Gaol, in the City of Hereford, for the murder of Walter Carwardine, on the night of Thursday, the 24th of March, 1831, Kent State University Libraries. Special Collections and Archives.

Bibliography

Burials at St Oswalds 1833–1839 (MF 108/9 Cheshire Records Office).

Cheshire Special Commission 25 May 1812. A Calendar of the Criminal Prisoners in the Custody of Matthew Hudson, Constable of His Majesty's Gaol, The Castle of Chester (HO 42/123 National Archives).

Chester Gaol Registers 1808–1865 (ZQAQ/3 Cheshire Record Office).

Cheshire Military Records 16th–19th Centuries for Henry Burrows (MG9/2 Cheshire Records Office).

Cheshire Military Records 16th–19th Centuries for Samuel Burrows (MG 8/6 Cheshire Records Office).

Convict Conduct Record, Charles Burrows (CON 31/1/1, Tasmania Libraries).

Copy of Verses on Samuel Thorley (Harding B 9/4 (245) John Johnson Collection, Bodleian Library, University of Oxford).

Death Warrant of Edith Morrey (QAB 5/8/10 Cheshire Record Office).

Death Warrant of John Lomas & Edith Morrey (QAB 5/8/9 Cheshire Record Office).

Death Warrant of James Mason (QAB 5/8/50 Cheshire Record Office).

Executions of criminals: more generally known by the uninviting name of 'Dying speeches'. Execution broadside (James Mason) (Harvard University 1834).

Griffith, Owen, a/ac John Jones. *Cerdd alarus, yn rhoddi hanes am Lewis Owen, yr hwn a ddienyddwyd ar Forfa Seiont, gerllaw Caerynarfon, ar ddydd Mercher Medi 4ydd, 1822: efe a garcharwyd am amcan lladd Mr. Sturdy (Supervisor), Conwy ... Cenir ar 'Fryniau'r Iwereddon/ [gan] Owain ap Cyffin, Migmint ; Meirion, a'i cant.* Llanrwst: Argraffwyd John Jones, 1825. Print. (The National Library of Wales).

Home Office: Domestic Correspondence, George III, Cheshire Special Commission, 25 May 1812 (HO-42-123 National Archives).

Indictment of John Carr of Barthomley for stabbing Thomas Horton (QAB 6/24 Cheshire Record Office).

Jones, John, a/ac John Jones. *Can newydd yn rhoddi hanes John Connor, Gwyddel 32 oed, yr hwn a ddienyddiwyd yn Rhuthun, Llun 15 Ebrill 1822, am yspeilio ac ymgais llofruddio, ar y ffordd rhwng Gwrecsam a Marchwiail/J. Jones, Treffynnon.* Trefriw: Argraffwyd gan J. Jones, 1822. Print. (The National Library of Wales).

Medical Journal of the *Princess Charlotte*, Convict Ship from 12 June to 1 December 1824. (National Archives ADM 101/61/6).

Muster Roll from *Princess Charlotte* for convict Charles Burrows (CON 13/1/3 Page 109, Tasmania Libraries).

Pigot and Co.'s Commercial Directory for Cheshire 1822–23.

Pigot and Co.'s Commercial Directory for Cheshire 1828–29.

Prisoners' Letters to the Bank of England, 1781–1827 [F25/1/145] Thomas Rushton, Giltspur Street Compter, 13 May 1802.

Reward poster for arson at William Radcliffe's warehouse (HO 40/1/1 National Archives).

Reports on criminals: correspondence: Report of W. Garrow on 1 individual petition (Matthew Hudson) on behalf of William Wilson. (HO 47/53/17 National Archives).

The Confession of James Lea (Shropshire Archives H 26.9 v.f).

The Fourth Report of The Committee Of the Society for the Improvement of Prison Discipline and the Reformation of Juvenile Offenders (T. Bentley, 1822).

The Trial at Large of John Lomas and Edith Morrey for Petit Treason … at Chester … the 21st Day of August 1812 (207013 Cheshire Record Office).

The Trial, Confession and Execution of James Lea and Joseph Grindley, who was Executed at Shrewsbury on Saturday, March 1832 (Shropshire Archives 665/4/605.

Books

Alexander, Alison, *Tasmania's Convicts: How Felons Built A Free Society* (Allen & Unwin, 2010).

Bailey, Victor (ed), *Policing and Punishment in Nineteenth Century Britain* (Routledge, 2016).

Bibliography

Baldwin, William & Knapp, Andrew, *The New Newgate Calendar: Being Interesting Memoirs of Notorious Characters, Who Have Been Convicted of Outrages on the Laws of England, During the Eighteenth Century, Brought Down to the Present Time, Volume 5* (Robins, 1830).

Banks, Stephen, *The British Execution* (Shire, 2013).

Boyce, James, *Van Diemen's Land* (Black Inc, 2008).

Brand, Emily, *The Georgian Bawdy House* (Shire, 2013).

Champness, John, *Thomas Harrison Georgian Architect of Chester and Lancaster, 1744–1829* (University of Lancaster, 2005).

Clarke, Richard, *Women and the Noose: A History of Female Execution* (The History Press, 2023).

Clifford, Naomi, *Women and the Gallows 1797–1837: Unfortunate Wretches* (Pen & Sword, 2017).

Corfield, Penelope, *The Georgians: The Deeds and Misdeeds of 18th Century Britain* (Yale University Press, 2022).

Dawson, Paul, *The Battle Against The Luddites: Unrest in The Industrial Revolution During The Napoleonic Wars* (Frontline, 2023).

Devereaux, Simon, *Execution, State and Society in England, 1660–1900* (Cambridge University Press, 2023).

Dobbs, Gary, *A Date With the Hangman* (Pen & Sword, 2019).

Eatwell, Alison, *Crime, Clemency & Consequence in Britain 1821–39: A Slice of Criminal Life* (Pen & Sword 2017).

Gatrell, Vic, *The Hanging Tree: Execution and the English People, 1770–1868* (Oxford University Press, 1994).

Griffin, Emma, *Liberty's Dawn: A People's History of the Industrial Revolution* (Yale University Press, 2013).

Hemingway, Joseph, *Panorama of the City of Chester* (T. Griffith, 1836).

Hobsbawn, Eric, *Captain Swing* (Phoenix, 2001).

Hobson, James, *Dark Days of Georgian Britain: Rethinking the Regency* (Pen & Sword, 2017).

Hughes, Margaret, *Crime and Punishment at Beaumaris* (Cwasg Carreg Gwalch, 2006).

Hughes, Thomas, *The Stranger's Handbook to Chester and its Environs* (E.J. Morton Re-published, 1972).

Hurley, Paul & Morgan, Len, *Chester Pubs* (Amberley, 2015).

Hurren, Elizabeth, *Dissecting the Criminal Corpse: Staging Post-Execution Punishment in Early Modern England* (Palgrave Macmillian, 2016).

Hutchinson, J.R., *The Press-Gang: Afloat and Ashore* (E.P. Dutton & Co., 1914).

Johnston, Helen, *Crime in England 1815–1830: Experiencing the Criminal Justice System* (Routledge, 2015).

King, Peter, *Punishing the Criminal Corpse, 1700–1840: Aggravated Forms of the Death Penalty in England* (Palgrave Macmillan, 2017).

Leigh, J., *Trial, Conviction and Execution of Samuel Fallowes, for the Wilful Murder of Betty Shawcross: Before Chief Justice Warren & Serjt Marshall, at Chester on Friday, April 11, 1823* (Leigh J., 1823).

Morrison, Robert, *The Regency Revolution: Jane Austen, Napoleon, Lord Byron and The Making of the Modern World* (Atlantic, 2019).

Newling, H., *A narrative of the fires which occurred in the parish of Whitchurch, Shropshire, in the years 1830 and 1831; together with an account of the trials of James Lea and Joseph Grindley, etc.* (Whitchurch, 1832).

Nield, Maureen, *Rope Dance: A Sensational Murder in Regency Cheshire Re-opened* (Cheshire County Council, 1993).

Pappalardo, Bruno, *How to Survive in The Georgian Navy: A Sailor's Guide* (Osprey, 2019).

Phillipson, Tacye, *Anatomy: A Matter of Death and Life* (NMSE – Publishing Ltd, 2022).

Sale, Kirkpatrick, *Rebels Against The Future: The Luddites And Their War On The Industrial Revolution: Lessons For The Computer Age* (Basic, 1996).

Seal, Graham, *Condemned: The Transported Men, Women and Children Who Built Britain's Empire* (Yale University Press, 2021).

Sly, Nicola, *Herefordshire Murders* (The History Press, 2010).

Tarlow, Sarah & Battell Lowman, Emma, *Harnessing the Power of the Criminal Corpse* (Palgrave Macmillian, 2018).

Wade, Stephen, *Britain's Most Notorious Hangmen* (Pen & Sword, 2009).
Ward, Simon, *Chester: A History* (The History Press, 2013).
Walliss, John, *The Bloody Code in England and Wales 1760–1830* (Palgrave Macmillaian, 2018).
Webb, Simon, *Execution: A History of Capital Punishment in Britain* (The History Press, 2011).
Wilkes, Sue, *Regency Cheshire* (Robert Hale, 2009).
Williams, Lucy, *Convicts in the Colonies: Transportation Tales from Britain to Australia* (Pen & Sword, 2018).
Wilson, Ben, *Decency & Disorder 1789–1837* (Faber & Faber, 2008).
Wood, Chris, *Famous Last Words: Confessions, Humour and Bravery of the Departing* (Pen & Sword, 2021).
Yarwood, Derek, *A Vintage Casebook of Cheshire Crime* (Derby, 2012).
Yarwood, Derek, *Cheshire's Execution Files* (Derby, 2011).
The Philanthropist, Or, Repository for Hints and Suggestions Calculated to Promote the Comfort and Happiness of Man: Volume 2. (Longman & Co., 1812).
Crime and Punishment in Chester (Chester Records Office, 1989).

Journal Articles

Handler, Phil, 'Forgery and the End of the "Bloody Code" in Early Nineteenth Century England' (*The Historical Journal* Vol. 48, No. 3).
Johnston, Helen, 'Discovering the Local Prison: Shrewsbury Gaol in the Nineteenth Century', (*The Local Historian* Vol. 35 No. 4).
McGowen, Randell, 'Managing the Gallows: The Bank of England and the Death Penalty, 1797–1821' (*Law and History Review* Vol. 25, No. 2).
Roberts, Matthew, 'Satan's Bank Note' (*History Today*, September 2017).
Walliss, John, 'Crime and Justice in Georgian Cheshire: The Chester Court of Great Sessions', 1760–1830 (*Journal of European History of Law* Vol. 6/ 2015 No. 1).

Newspapers

Chester Chronicle and Cheshire and North Wales Advertiser
Chester Courant
Englishman
English Chronicle and Whitehall Evening Post
Hereford Journal
Illustrated Sporting News and Theatrical and Musical Review
Kentish Weekly Post or Canterbury Journal
Knutsford Guardian
Liverpool Albion
London Packet and New Lloyd's Evening Post
Lancaster Gazette
Manchester Mercury
Morning Herald
National Register
Northwich Guardian
Salopian Journal
Staffordshire Advertiser
Stockport Advertiser
The Sun (London)
The Spectator
Warrington Guardian

Websites

https://chester.shoutwiki.com/wiki/Execution_at_Chester
https://chesterwalls.info/
www.capitalpunishmentuk.org
https://convictrecords.com.au/
https://www.britishnewspaperarchive.co.uk/
https://curiosity.lib.harvard.edu/crime-broadsides

Bibliography

https://ludditebicentenary.blogspot.com/
https://libcom.org/article/luddites-war-industry-story-machine-smashing-and-spies
www.regencyhistory.net
www.historicengland.org.uk/
www.prisonhistory.org

Index

1751 Murder Act 31, 50

Addington, Henry (Home Secretary) 99
Allen, Joseph 73–75, 77–82
Allen Samuel 79
Allender, George (Sheriff of Chester) 138–139

Bank of England 73–78
Bawdy House 94
Beaumaris ix, 142–144, 147, 150–151
   Beaumaris Gaol 144, 149
   Griffith, William 141–142, 144–149
   Griffith, Mary 144–145
Bellyse, John (Surgeon) 44
Birchall, Captain William 63–67
Bock, Teddy (Ballad Singer/Writer) 47–48
Bowers, Thomas (Sheriff of Chester) 138–139
Burgess, William 56–57, 59–60

Burrows, Charles 5, 17, 39, 122–127, 139, 175–176
Burrows, Henry 5, 17, 39, 61, 63–65, 110, 122, 126, 133, 139, 175–176
Burrows, Mary (nee Williams) 5, 10–11, 15–16, 24, 58, 61, 63–65, 68, 80, 97, 98, 110, 118, 120–122, 126, 128–130, 135, 151, 169, 175–177
Burrows, Samuel (Hangman):
   Beadle 11–12, 20, 62, 119, 177
   Beaumaris 142–143, 147
   Beaumaris Gaol 149
   Butcher 4, 10, 13, 17, 39, 54, 56, 61, 65, 121, 131, 141
   Birth 10
   Breaking The Peace 176–177
   Brook Street 1–2, 6, 129–130, 134–135, 140, 143, 151, 169
   Burial 179
   Carnarvon (now Caernarfon) 98–100
   Chester Castle 19, 33, 79, 98, 103, 105, 110–111

Index

Conversion and Death of
  Samuel Burrows 179
Death 178
Drinking (Alcohol consumption)
  3, 11, 85, 99, 131, 133, 159,
  169, 173, 176, 178
Height 39
Hereford 150, 153–154,
  155–156, 158
Marriage 10
New City Gaol 3, 13, 38, 49,
  52, 58, 71, 84, 96, 111–112,
  117, 119–120, 134–136, 170,
  174, 180
Northgate Street 4, 10, 15–16,
  18, 24, 37, 55, 56, 61–62, 64,
  86, 104–105, 110, 117, 121,
  128, 130–131, 133, 143, 169
Portrait 2
Press Gang 64–65, 72, 175
Rat Catching 130–131, 151, 177
Ravensmoor 10
Red Lion (Ruthin) 89
Retainer 33, 80, 85, 104, 132,
  141–143, 151, 177
Ruthin 85–87, 92
Shambles 4, 10, 13, 17, 19,
  37, 54, 56, 61, 64, 65, 121,
  131–132
Shrewsbury 159, 160, 164

Caddock, Henry 90
Carey, Rev. Francis Lucius 62–66
Carr, John 168, 171, 173, 176
Challinor, William 168
City of Chester:
  Abbey Street 27
  Abbey Square 27
  Brook Street 1, 2, 6, 129–130,
    134–135, 140, 143, 151, 169
  Bridge Street 2, 19, 20, 27, 47,
    59, 64, 69, 81, 168
  Chester Castle (County
    Goal) 16–17, 19, 22, 29, 32,
    33, 37, 45, 46, 51, 68, 75,
    79, 95, 96, 98, 103, 105, 107,
    110–111, 115, 125, 136, 137,
    159, 161, 163, 171–172
  Chester Chronicle
    (Newspaper) 40, 111, 123,
    132, 145
  Chester Courant (Newspaper)
    2, 96, 113–115, 180
  Chester Corporation 27, 52,
    169, 177
  Coach & Horses 169
  Cottage Tavern 130, 169, 177
  Crown & Mitre 169
  Dublin Packet 15, 169
  Exchange 4, 12, 27, 86, 98,
    117–120, 151
  Foregate Street 15
  Gloverstone 38, 69, 70, 81,
    96, 105
  Golden Eagle 54, 80
  Handbridge 15, 179

King Street 69, 143
New City Gaol 3, 6, 12–13,
    15–18, 22, 25–27, 29, 32, 37,
    38, 40–41, 44, 46, 48–50,
    52, 56, 58–59, 61, 69–71,
    73, 84–85, 93, 96, 104–105,
    111–113, 117, 119–120,
    134–136, 143, 159, 168, 169,
    173–174, 177, 180
Nicholas Street 111
Northgate Gaol 12, 16–18
Northgate Street 4, 10, 15–16,
    18, 19, 24, 27, 37, 55–56,
    61, 62, 64, 86, 104–105, 110,
    117–118, 121, 128, 130–131,
    133, 143, 169
Old King's Head 168
Pied Bull 62
Roodee Racecourse 18, 26, 31,
    93, 166
St. Oswald's (Parish) 11, 20,
    62, 177, 179
Watergate Street 19, 20, 48, 50,
    59–60, 69–70, 135, 166
White Lion Hotel 98–99
Caldecot, William Lloyd 99, 102
Clare, John 18
Clarke, Rev. William 5–8, 84,
    134–135, 138, 140, 178, 179
Coups, Mary 106, 108
Crawley, Peter (Boxer) 94–95
Cumberledge, James 159–160,
    163–166

Dallas, Judge Robert 44–46,
    50, 58
Davenport, William (Bramall
    Hall) 105
Davenport, William (Sheriff of
    Chester) 119
Dobie, John (Surgeon–
    Superintendent *Princess
    Charlotte*) 127
Dooley, William 43–44
Done, Thomas 26–28, 30–31, 49
Ducker, Edward 119

Eckersley, Betty 28–29
Evans, Hannah 42

Fallows, Samuel 104–112
Frodsham 57

Garrow, Sir William (Chief Justice
    of Chester) 79
Garside, Thomas 36
Glover, George 15–16, 19,
    20–25, 39
Glover, Thomas (Inspector of
    Notes) 74, 78
Goodair, John 35–36
Groom, George 93, 95
Groom, John 43

Hanmer 88
Harrison, George (Mayor of
    Chester) 174

Index

Harrison, Thomas (Architect) 12, 16, 28, 143, 161
Henry VII (Great Charter) 70
Henshall, John 134–135, 137–140
Hereford ix, 150–156, 158
   Carwardine, Walter 152–157
   Carwardine, William 155, 157
   Coley, Sarah 152–153
   Connop, Susan 151–153, 155, 157
   Hereford Gaol 150, 155
   Matthews, John 150, 153
   Pugh Joseph 150, 152–153, 155–158
   Quaker's Lane 152–153, 154
   Reignart, Susan 152–153
   Williams, Mary Ann 156–157
   Williams, William 150, 153–154, 156–157
Hobart 127–128
Hobart Penitentiary 128
Holland, Hannah 46
Holroyd, Robert 28
Howard, John (Reformer) 161
Howell, James (Watchman) 63
Hudson, Matthew (Constable of the County Gaol in Chester) 32–33, 45–46, 68–69
Humphreys, Captain Salusbury Pryce 108

Jackson, Daniel 64
Jelly, Joseph 79

Jones, William (Stall Trader) 124–125
Jones, W.C. (Printer) 69
Justitia Hulk 125–126

Kragon, John 113–117

Lawton Salt Works 21
Lloyd, Mary 75–78
Luddites 32, 35, 37–8, 160
Lymm 28–9
Lomas, John 32, 41–43, 45–47, 49, 52–53

Mackintosh, Sir James 116
Mansfield, James (Chief Justice for Chester) 75
Mary I 17
Marsh, George 17
Mason, James 168, 170–71, 173, 176
Massey, William (Mayor of Chester) 115, 117, 119
Meredith, Sir William 116
Morrey, Edith 32, 41–43, 45–46, 49, 51–53, 55, 58–59, 71
Morrey, George 32, 42–45
Morrey, Thomas 51

Naylor, William 168, 171, 173, 176

Owen, Lewis 98–102

Peel, Robert (Home Secretary) 114, 116–17, 120, 130, 137

Porter, Mary 56–57
Press Gang 63–66, 72
Princess Charlotte 126, 127
Proudlove, John 136
Proudlove, William 15–16,
   19–25, 39

Radcliffe, William 35
Ravensmoor 4, 10, 56
Riley, Thomas 168, 171, 173, 176
Roby, Thomas 131–2
Romilly, Sir Samuel 116
Rowlands, Griffith (Surgeon)
   26–9, 31, 49
Runcorn 28, 57
Rushton, Thomas 76
Ruthin ix, 83, 85–9, 91–5
   Connor, John 83, 85, 87–92
   Galltegfa 83, 91
   Jones, John (Ballad
     Writer) 88–9
   Ruthin Gaol 87, 90–1
   Thomas, William 88–9

St. Helens 56–7
Shawcross, Betty 106, 108–109
Shrewsbury xi, 160, 164
   Grindley, Joseph 159, 161–4

Lea, James 159, 161–4
Shrewsbury Gaol 159
Swing Riots 160
Stockport 34–35

Temples, John 32, 37–40
Thompson, Joseph 32, 36–40
Thorley, Samuel 168, 171–173
Titley, Owen (Surgeon) 26–29, 31,
   49, 50–51, 53–55
Tongue, William 93, 95–97

Van Dieman's Land 5, 22, 33, 37,
   76, 79, 125, 126, 127, 128, 130,
   138, 164, 176

Wagstaff, Samuel 37
Waltham Black Act 21, 141
Whittle, Thomas
   (Ropemaker) 143
Wilson, William 61, 63–68, 80
Wilkinson, William 56–57, 59
Woodhouse, Joseph 134–139
Workhouse (House of
   Industry) 166
Wrexham 88–89, 123

Yarwood, James 56–57, 59–60